T0356153

VIRGINIA
in the
AMERICAN REVOLUTION

VIRGINIA
in the
AMERICAN REVOLUTION

CHARLES A. MILLS

THE
History
PRESS

Published by The History Press
Charleston, SC
www.historypress.com

Dedicated to our Patriot ancestors.

CONTENTS

PREFACE

One of the difficulties about understanding the American Revolution is that after 250 years, the people no longer seem real to us. It has been said that the past is like a foreign country—they do things differently there. Our technology is different, our attitudes are different and our beliefs are different, yet we still share a common humanity with the people of the past. The people who lived 250 years ago had the same passions, strengths and weaknesses that we have today. They weren't worse and they weren't better. But they were different, and they ordered their lives very differently.

Here we present the political and military aspects of the American Revolution in Virginia, but we also present the day-to-day social reality of the people of Virginia at the time, how they lived and how they ordered their lives. We also present little-known stories of the Revolution, such as the plot to kidnap Benedict Arnold, the personal woes of George Washington and the midnight ride of the Paul Revere of Virginia. And then there are the stories of extraordinary women and the dilemma of enslaved people.

History is nothing more than the story of people living day in and day out, interacting with one another for good or ill. History is complicated because people are complicated. Our lives are connected to everyone who has ever lived and to everyone who will ever live in the future. What we do every day is important in this unending chain of cause and effect. There are no ordinary moments. Another 250 years from now, the people of the twenty-third century will be throwing rocks at those who lived in the twenty-first century. This should make us both humble because we have a long way to go to fulfill the dream of America and hopeful because we have come a long way toward realizing it.

One of the first things we must do to understand the people of the Revolutionary era is to put things into perspective. Today, the United States has a population of some 300 million. The thirteen colonies had a population of 3 million, of whom approximately 20 percent were enslaved. Britain had a population of 7 million, so some might wonder how the British thought they would be able subdue the colonies. The answer is simple: the colonists were divided. Approximately one-third were in favor of revolution, a third were in favor of the king and a third were on the fence waiting to see what the final outcome would be. Total American casualties (primarily from sickness and disease) during the entire war from 1775 to 1783 amounted to some 25,000. This may seem an insignificant number compared to casualties in the Civil War of the 1860s (600,000) or to those of World War II (405,000), but as a percentage of total population, 25,000 dead during the Revolution represents a modern equivalent of 2.5 million dead. The sacrifices were great and the stakes were high. Virginia, as the richest and most populous colony, provided the military genius, the political wisdom and the physical and material resources that brought final victory.

Many fine historians and history enthusiasts have shared their insights and knowledge with me. I highly recommend *The Revolution in Virginia, 1775–1783* by John Selby and *A Universal Appearance of War* by Michael Cecere for their detailed and masterful treatments of the political and military aspects of the Revolution in Virginia. I want to especially thank my son, Andrew L. Mills, who has a true passion for eighteenth-century history; Professor Jane Turner Censer with George Mason University; George Washington's Mount Vernon estate; Ross Schwalm, the greatest Hessian of them all; Don Francisco, America's greatest fifer; Richard Potter for making me aware of the importance of the Revolution in bringing about religious freedom; and the Sons of the American Revolution (SAR) and the Daughters of the American Revolution (DAR) for their tireless efforts in keeping the ideals of the Revolution evergreen.

PART I

THE EVENTS OF THE AMERICAN REVOLUTION IN VIRGINIA

THE COMING STORM, 1763–1773

John Carlyle, of Alexandria, stands out as representative of the type of person who sought to make a life and a fortune in the colony of Virginia. Carlyle came to Virginia in 1741, at the age of twenty-one, as the agent of a merchant in hopes of making "a fortune sufficient…to live independent." He achieved success within seven years. Carlyle's extensive business activities included import and export trade to England and the West Indies, retail trade in Alexandria, an iron foundry in the Shenandoah Valley, milling and a blacksmithing operation. Carlyle bought thousands of acres of land and operated three working plantations. In 1749, Carlyle became one of the founding fathers of Alexandria. In 1753, he built a grand home in Alexandria overlooking the Potomac River. Carlyle used slave labor in all of his business ventures. Enslaved people toiled on his plantations, sailed his ships and hauled his goods. Slave carpenters and masons were used to build his mansion. If Carlyle had any reservations about slavery, he did not voice them.

Like many of his contemporaries, John Carlyle's antagonism toward Great Britain began in 1755 during the French and Indian War. While the majority of people in the American colonies identified themselves as loyal Englishmen throughout most of the eighteenth century, the British looked down on America as a wilderness inhabited by a motley mix of renegades, malcontents, criminals, slaves and Indians, unable to produce manufactured goods for itself and culturally primitive. Appointed commissary of the Virginia militia in 1755, John Carlyle had a close view of the British attitude and complained that the British troops "by some means or another came in so prejudiced against us [and] our Country... that they used us like an enemy country and took everything they wanted and paid nothing, or very little, for it. And when complaints [were] made to the commanding officers, they [cursed] the country and inhabitants, calling us the spawn of convicts the sweepings of the gaols...which made their company very disagreeable."

With the end of the French and Indian War in 1763 and the final removal of the foreign threat, the deterioration of relations between Great Britain and the colonies accelerated. Faced with a huge debt because of its prolonged war against the French, the British Parliament passed a number of tax bills that directly levied new taxes on the American colonies. In 1764, Parliament passed the Sugar Act and in 1765 the Stamp Act. The people of Virginia, like those in the other American colonies, rejected Parliament's right to impose new taxes on America.

On May 29, 1765, Patrick Henry of Hanover County passionately addressed the Virginia House of Burgesses urging the adoption of what are known as the Virginia Resolves. Henry thundered, "Caesar had his Brutus, Charles I his Cromwell, and George III [here his speech was interrupted by cries of "Treason! Treason!"]...may profit by their example. If this be treason, make the most of it!"

The Virginia Resolves were adopted by the House of Burgesses (the fifth resolve was deleted after Patrick Henry left Williamsburg for home):

> RESOLVED, *that the first adventurers and settlers of His Majesty's colony and dominion of Virginia brought with them and transmitted to their posterity, and all other His Majesty's subjects since inhabiting in this His Majesty's said colony, all the liberties, privileges, franchises, and immunities that have at any time been held, enjoyed, and possessed by the people of Great Britain.*

> RESOLVED, *that by two royal charters, granted by King James I, the colonists aforesaid are declared entitled to all liberties, privileges, and immunities of denizens and natural subjects to all intents and purposes as if they had been abiding and born within the Realm of England.*

> RESOLVED, *that the taxation of the people by themselves, or by persons chosen by themselves to represent them, who can only know what taxes the people are able to bear, or the easiest method of raising them, and must themselves be affected by every tax laid on the people, is the only security against a burdensome taxation, and the distinguishing characteristic of British freedom, without which the ancient constitution cannot exist.*

> RESOLVED, *that His Majesty's liege people of this his most ancient and loyal colony have without interruption enjoyed the inestimable right of being governed by such laws, respecting their internal policy and taxation, as are derived from their own consent, with the approbation of their sovereign, or his substitute; and that the same has never been forfeited or yielded up, but has been constantly recognized by the kings and people of Great Britain.*

> RESOLVED, *therefor that the General Assembly of this Colony have the only and exclusive Right and Power to lay Taxes and Impositions upon the inhabitants of this Colony and that every Attempt to vest such Power in any person or persons whatsoever other than the General Assembly aforesaid has a manifest Tendency to destroy British as well as American Freedom.*

The royal governor, Francis Fauquier, reacted by dissolving the assembly, but the spirit of resistance was still noticeable abroad. The Northampton County court unilaterally declared the Stamp Act null and void. The Sons of Liberty, a loosely organized secret organization, met and encouraged protests. Richard Bland penned a powerful pamphlet titled *An Enquiry into the Rights of the British Colonies* in which he made the point that under the unwritten British constitution, dependent as it was on precedents, Virginia, although part of the British empire, was not part of the kingdom of Great Britain. Virginia, therefore, owed allegiance only to the king and not to the British Parliament. It was a fine legal and scholarly argument, soon boiled down to the more understandable, "No taxation without representation," which became the watchword phrase not only in Virginia but throughout the other American colonies as well.

Not all protests were peaceful. Archibald McCall insisted on obeying the letter of the law, collecting the requisite tax that Parliament placed on stamps and other documents. A mob descended on McCall's home in Tappahannock, Virginia. Rocks shattered the windows. McCall was dragged out and promptly tarred and feathered.

The British Parliament repealed the Stamp Act in 1766 but imposed new revenue acts. The underlying problem was unresolved. Parliament insisted on its right of taxing the Americans, but the Americans were having none of it.

On March 12, 1773, the Virginia House of Burgesses created a permanent Committee of Correspondence in order to coordinate with the other colonies in measures opposing the overreach of the British Parliament. Ultimately, however, it was the so-called Boston Tea Party of December 16, 1773, that crystalized opinion throughout the American colonies. On the evening of December 16, 1773, some one hundred men, some disguised as Mohawk warriors, boarded three ships in Boston Harbor and dumped ninety-two thousand pounds of tea into the water.

Samuel Adams of Massachusetts argued that this was not the act of a lawless mob, but was instead a principled protest and that the only remaining option the people had to defend their constitutional rights. His cousin John Adams wrote, "This is the most magnificent Movement of all. There is a Dignity, a Majesty, a Sublimity, in this last Effort of the Patriots that I greatly admire. The People should never rise, without doing something to be remembered—something notable And striking. This Destruction of the Tea is so bold, so daring, so firm, intrepid and inflexible, and it must have so important Consequences, and so lasting, that I can't but consider it as an Epocha in History."

The issue of "who rules?" was now well and truly on the table.

The War of Words, 1774–1775

News of the Boston Tea Party reached England in January 1774. The British prime minister, Lord North, told Parliament, "The Americans have tarred and feathered your subjects, plundered your merchants, burnt your ships, denied all obedience to your laws and authority; yet so clement and so long forbearing has our conduct been that it is incumbent on us now to take a different course. Whatever may be the consequences, we must risk something; if we do not, all is over."

Parliament passed three acts designed to bring Massachusetts under control. The Boston Port Act closed the port of Boston until the colonists paid for the destroyed tea and the British government was satisfied that order had been restored.

The Massachusetts Government Act revoked the colony's charter and placed Massachusetts under the direct control of the British government. Even town meetings were limited to one per year. Virginians and other American colonists now feared that Parliament could unilaterally change the structure of their government without their consent.

The Administration of Justice Act allowed the royal governor to change the trial venue of any royal official whom the governor did not think could get a fair trial in the colony of Massachusetts. Virginians thought that this act established a dangerous precedent. George Washington labeled it the "Murder Act" because he strongly believed that it would allow British officials to abuse Americans and escape justice.

Many Virginians regarded the acts as intolerable violations of their constitutional rights, their natural rights and their colonial charters. Richard Henry Lee of Virginia described the acts as "a most wicked System for destroying the liberty of America."

The Royal Navy began patrolling the mouth of Boston Harbor. British troops under the command of General Thomas Gage filled the streets of Boston. Virginians and other colonists sent relief supplies to the people of Massachusetts.

In May, the Virginia House of Burgesses approved June 1, 1774, as a day of "Fasting, Humiliation, and Prayer" in support of the people of Massachusetts. Virginia's royal governor, John Murray, Earl of Dunmore, dissolved the legislature, but in an act of defiance, the burgesses reconvened on May 27 in the Apollo room of the Raleigh Tavern in Williamsburg. The burgesses called on Virginia counties to elect delegates to a special convention to be held in August.

Citizens of Fairfax County met in Alexandria's courthouse on July 18, 1774, where they approved a document, largely written by George Mason, known as the Fairfax Resolves. The Fairfax Resolves identified American rights and declared the determination of the people to defend them. George Washington was one of the delegates chosen to carry the Fairfax Resolves to the First Virginia Convention, held in Williamsburg on August 1, 1774. A most vital portion of the Fairfax Resolves stated, "Resolved that the most important part of the British Constitution is the fundamental Principle of the People's being governed by no Laws, to which they have not given their Consent. For if this Part of the Constitution was taken away, the Government must degenerate into an absolute and despotic Monarchy and the freedom of the people be annihilated." More than thirty counties in Virginia passed similar resolutions in 1774. Such resolutions as those from Virginia served as the jumping-off place for the deliberations of the First Continental Congress, convened in Philadelphia on September 5, 1774, to coordinate an overall colonial response to the Port Act and the other Coercive Acts. Peyton Randolph of Virginia was elected president of the First Continental Congress.

The Second Virginia Convention was convened at St. John's Episcopal Church in Richmond on March 20, 1775. At this convention, Patrick Henry, a delegate from Hanover County, proposed raising a Virginia militia independent of royal authority. His harsh language about the inevitability of war with Britain enraged moderates, sparking heated opposition. On March 23, Patrick Henry defended his proposal:

> *If we were base enough to desire it, it is now too late to retire from the contest. There is no retreat but in submission and slavery! Our chains are forged! Their clanking may be heard on the plains of Boston! The war is inevitable and let it come! I repeat it, sir, let it come. It is in vain, sir, to extenuate the matter. Gentlemen may cry, Peace, Peace but there is no peace. The war is actually begun! The next gale that sweeps from the north will bring to our ears the clash of resounding arms! Our brethren are already in the field! Why stand we here idle? What is it that gentlemen wish? What would they have? Is life so dear, or peace so sweet, as to be purchased at the price of chains and slavery? Forbid it, Almighty God! I know not what course others may take; but as for me, give me liberty or give me death!*

It should be noted that although this is the popularly accepted version of Patrick Henry's speech, no verbatim transcript was made at the time. The speech as it has come down to us was reconstructed some twenty years later from accounts of people who heard the speech. In any event, all who heard it agreed that the speech was "one of the boldest, vehement, and animated pieces of eloquence that had ever been delivered." Patrick Henry swayed the opinion of the delegates, who voted to put the colony into a posture of defense.

One month later, Royal Navy sailors under the direction of the governor, Lord Dunmore, arrived in Williamsburg with the intention of removing all of the gunpowder from the public magazine and transporting it to the British ship HMS *Magdalen*. Townspeople discovered what was happening and raised an alarm. An incensed crowd gathered and faced the governor and his servants, who were now armed with muskets. Town officers demanded the return of the powder, claiming that it was the property of the colony to which the royal governor had no right. Lord Dunmore said that he had

At St. John's Episcopal Church in Richmond, Patrick Henry thundered, "Give me liberty, or give me death!" *Courtesy of the Library of Congress.*

learned of a planned slave uprising and was removing the powder for reasons of public safety. The Speaker of the House of Burgesses, Peyton Randolph, calmed the situation, at least for the moment.

Suspicions of the governor's motives persisted. On April 22, after a second angry crowd, fully capable of storming the governor's palace, was convinced to disperse by local leaders, Lord Dunmore angrily declared that if attacked he would "declare freedom to the slaves, and reduce the city of Williamsburg to ashes."

By April 29, militiamen all over Virginia had learned about the battles in Massachusetts at Lexington and Concord on April 19. Hundreds of men mustered at Fredericksburg and decided to send a messenger to Williamsburg before marching on the capital. Once again, Peyton Randolph sought to prevent violence and urged restraint. The militiamen at Fredericksburg voted not to march. But there were others who were more hotheaded. On May 2, the Hanover County militia, led by Patrick Henry, voted to march on Williamsburg. On May 3, Patrick Henry and the militia were fifteen miles from Williamsburg. Lord Dunmore and his family departed for the governor's hunting lodge, Porto Bello, and from there to HMS *Fowey* at anchor in the York River.

Lord Dunmore arrived in Williamsburg with the intention of removing all of the gunpowder from the public magazine. *Courtesy of the Library of Congress.*

Moderates were still looking for ways to ease tensions. Carter Braxton, a moderate member of the House of Burgesses, came up with a solution. Braxton negotiated a settlement with royal officials such that the colony would receive payment for the gunpowder. On May 4, Patrick Henry received a full bill of exchange, signed by an intermediary (a wealthy planter), as payment for the powder. A triumphant Patrick Henry then set off for Philadelphia to take his place as a Virginia delegate to the Second Continental Congress, where he presented the payment to the other Virginia delegates at the Congress.

On May 6, Lord Dunmore issued a proclamation charging that the money had been extorted and that "a certain Patrick Henry and a number of deluded followers who had organized an independent company and put themselves in a posture of war be arrested as traitors."

Still trying to assert his authority, Lord Dunmore returned to Williamsburg on May 12. He called the House of Burgesses together in early June to consider a Conciliatory Resolution offered by the British prime minister. Lord North laid before the House of Commons a resolution proposing that whenever any colonial assembly agreed to make a grant for the common defense and the support of civil government in the colony (such grants to be "disposable by Parliament"), the British government would forbear to impose on that colony any other tax or assessment for these purposes.

The British proposal was sent to each of the colonies separately and was seen as a trick to divide the colonies and bypass the Continental Congress. The House of Burgesses rejected the proposal, as did the Continental Congress in no uncertain terms:

> *The Congress took the said resolution into consideration, and are, thereupon, of opinion, That colonies of America are entitled to the sole and exclusive privilege of giving and granting their own money.... To propose, therefore, as this resolution does, that the monies given by the colonies shall be subject to the disposal of parliament alone, is to, propose that they shall relinquish this right of enquiry, and put it in the power of others to render their gifts ruinous, in proportion as they are liberal.... The proposition seems also to have been calculated more particularly to lull into fatal security, our well-affected fellow-subjects on the other side the water, till time should be given for the operation of those arms, which a British minister pronounced would instantaneously reduce the "cowardly" sons of America to unreserved submission. But, when the world reflects, how inadequate to justice are these vaunted terms; when it attends to the rapid and bold succession of injuries, which, during the course of eleven years, have been aimed at these colonies; when it reviews the pacific and respectful expostulations, which, during that whole time, were the sole arms we opposed to them; when it observes that our complaints were either not heard at all, or were answered with new and accumulated injuries; when it recollects that the minister himself, on an early occasion, declared, "that he would never treat with America, till he had brought her to his feet," and that an avowed partisan of* [the] *ministry has more lately denounced against us the dreadful sentence, "delenda est Carthago"* ["Carthage must be destroyed"]; *that this was done in presence of a British Senate and being unreproved by them, must be taken to be their own sentiment (especially as the purpose has already in part been carried into execution, by their treatment of Boston and burning of Charlestown); when it considers the great armaments with which they have invaded us, and the circumstances of cruelty with which these have commenced and prosecuted hostilities; when these things, we say, are laid together and attentively considered, can the world be deceived into an opinion that we are unreasonable, or can it hesitate to believe with us, that nothing but our own exertions may defeat the ministerial sentence of death or abject submission?*

FROM WORDS TO WAR, 1775–1776

On June 8, 1775, as animosity toward Britain continued to grow, Lord Dunmore left Williamsburg and took refuge aboard HMS *Fowey*, apparently washing his hands of the obstinate House of Burgesses. The colony was now without an active executive. This was remedied in July when the Third Virginia Convention convened in Richmond. The convention created a Committee of Safety to govern as an executive body in the absence of the royal governor. The convention also divided Virginia into sixteen military districts and resolved to raise regular regiments.

Although the royal governor had abandoned Williamsburg and thousands of militiamen were preparing for war, there was no armed conflict during the summer of 1775. Each side was trying to improve its military posture. The Virginians collected arms and ammunition and drilled their units. The royal governor enlisted Loyalists and petitioned General Gage to send troops from Boston. Eventually, General Gage sent some two hundred British regulars from the Fourteenth Regiment of Foot. With his augmented forces, Lord Dunmore began making forays into the countryside to confiscate militia arms and ammunition. During the first raid, staged on October 12, Lord Dunmore seized nineteen cannons of various sizes, seventeen of which were immediately destroyed, while two were taken away. More successful raids followed, causing Lord Dunmore to inform British military authorities that "landing in this manner has discouraged exceedingly the Rebels, and has raised the Spirits of the friends of Government so much that they are offering their Services from all quarters."

As royalist strength increased, British raids became even bolder. On October 26, Captain Matthew Squire anchored a squadron of four small British naval vessels off Hampton. His was a mission of retaliation for the burning of a small British tender by the people of Hampton two months before. Captain Squire intended to burn the town to the ground. He had not, however, counted on resistance. No one knows who fired the first shot. Lord Dunmore blamed Captain George Nichols of the Second Virginia Regiment. The Virginians insisted that the British opened fire first. Skirmishing lasted for two days, resulting in the deaths of two British sailors. War had come to Virginia.

On November 7, Lord Dunmore declared martial law and issued a proclamation declaring Virginia to be in a state of rebellion. The proclamation offered freedom to any slave (belonging to a rebel) who fought for the British in putting down the rebellion. The House of Burgesses decided that Lord

Lord Dunmore took refuge with the British fleet, washing his hands of the obstinate House of Burgesses. *Courtesy of the Library of Congress.*

Dunmore's prolonged absence constituted his resignation. Virginia was now officially under the political leadership of the Committee of Safety established by the Third Virginia Convention. Meanwhile, Virginia's ablest soldier, George Washington, was in the North, having been appointed head of American forces by the Continental Congress.

Lord Dunmore was able to recruit enough enslaved men seeking freedom to form what he called the Ethiopian Regiment. Initially, the regiment was three hundred strong. He also raised a force of Loyalists he designated the Queen's Own Loyal Virginia Regiment. With these local forces and the British regulars of the Fourteenth Regiment of Foot at his command, Lord Dunmore could write on November 30, 1775, that he would soon be able to "reduce this colony to a proper sense of their duty." The claim was made all the more believable since Lord Dunmore's forces had routed rebel militia at Kemp's Landing two weeks earlier. There inexperienced militiamen, fighting in the open, opened fire too early. The disciplined British regulars returned fire and moved quickly through the woods with their fearsome fifteen-inch bayonets, flushing out the rebels. The militia fled without further resistance. In total, eighteen rebels were captured and seven were killed. One British soldier suffered a minor wound.

Lord Dunmore, now operating from a British ship off the town of Norfolk, ordered the fortification of the bridge across the southern branch of the Elizabeth River nine miles south of Norfolk at a village known as Great Bridge. The bridge was on the only road leading south from Norfolk toward North Carolina. If Norfolk was to be supplied and not fall into the hands of the rebels, it was essential that this road be defended. A stockade fort was built and garrisoned by some eighty men.

Meanwhile, realizing the importance of not allowing Lord Dunmore to fortify Norfolk for use as a base of operations, the Virginians had not been idle. Four hundred men of the Second Virginia Regiment and one hundred riflemen from the Culpeper Minutemen set up camp across from the British fort at Great Bridge on December 2. The Virginians, under the command of William Woodford, overestimated the strength of the enemy and began entrenching, awaiting the arrival of more militia companies from Virginia and neighboring North Carolina. By December 9, there were some nine hundred men facing the British and Loyalists, who numbered half of this force. Some cannons had also arrived with the men from North Carolina, but they were useless because they lacked mountings and carriages.

Now Lord Dunmore would fall victim to the fog of war. Learning that the rebel militia had cannons (but unaware that they were inoperable); underestimating the number of the enemy, which he thought less than his own; and having little respect for the military prowess of the militia, Lord Dunmore decided that the best defense was an offense. Lord Dunmore's plan called for a diversionary attack by the Ethiopian Regiment at a spot downriver from the bridge to draw the militia's attention, while an assault force, made up primarily of British regulars, would attack across the bridge in the early morning. Because of a series of muddled orders, the planned diversionary attack never occurred. The forces inside the fort nevertheless decided to attack across the bridge.

Captain Charles Fordyce of the Fourteenth Regiment of Foot led some 120 British regulars across the bridge, brushing aside the militia sentries. Fordyce's men were joined by navy gunners operating field artillery supporting the attack. Loyalist companies stood ready on the fort side of the bridge to follow up a successful assault by the British regulars.

A militia company numbering about sixty prepared for the British advance behind earthworks, some four hundred yards from the main rebel camp. The British regulars marched forward six abreast, advancing with fixed bayonets. The militiamen withheld fire until the British were within fifty yards and then let loose a withering fire. The British advance stalled and then dissolved as the militia musket fire continued. Half of the assaulting force was killed, and many were wounded.

Colonel Woodford and the entire rebel force were now marching out to attack the British. The British naval gunners spiked their guns and fled across the bridge. Colonel Woodford ordered the riflemen of the Culpeper Minutemen, whose weapons had a much longer range than standard muskets, to begin firing on the Loyalist forces on the far side of the bridge. The British field commander, Captain Leslie, ordered his men to retreat into the fort. Fearing that the rebels were now in a position to take the fort, Captain Leslie abandoned the fort that night under the cover of darkness and marched the shaken garrison to Norfolk.

It was a stunning victory for the American forces. Colonel Woodford described it in a letter to the *Virginia Gazette* of December 15: "This was a second Bunker's Hill affair, in miniature; with this difference, that we kept our post, and had only one man wounded in the hand."

In the aftermath of the battle, Captain Leslie dispatched the British regulars to royal naval vessels. Lord Dunmore's Loyalist supporters, unnerved by the rebel victory, also sought refuge on the ships. Reinforced by hundreds of additional troops from North Carolina, Colonel Woodford occupied Norfolk on December 14.

The British ships remained anchored off Norfolk. Lord Dunmore tried to negotiate with the Virginians for water and provisions. These overtures were rebuffed. British landing parties in search of water and provisions were repulsed. Random shots were fired at the fleet, and the Virginians regularly taunted the British. On January 1, 1776, the fleet retaliated. The *Virginia Gazette* reported, "It was a shocking scene to see the poor women and children running about through the fire, and exposed to the guns from the ships, and some of them with children at their breasts. Let our countrymen view and contemplate the scene. The cannonade lasted twenty five hours…and the flames were raging and had consumed two thirds of the town.…It is affirmed that one hundred cannon played on the town almost incessantly for twenty five hours."

Norfolk was now a smoking ruin. After a wet and miserable January, both sides decamped. Rebel forces abandoned Norfolk on February 6, burning the remaining buildings as they departed. The British sailed away and took up positions around Portsmouth. The danger Lord Dunmore posed to the rebel cause had not been eliminated. George Washington, commander-in-chief of the Continental army, wrote a letter to General Charles Lee, who had been sent to take command of troops in the South, warning of continued danger: "[I]f that Man is not crushed before Spring, he will become the most formidable Enemy America has....[N]othing less than depriving him of life or liberty will secure peace to Virginia."

Although Lord Dunmore was as savage as ever and might well have wished to rain fire and death on the rebels, the tide had definitely turned. While Lord Dunmore struggled to recruit men, the Virginians were having no problem filling the ranks. The biggest problem the Virginians now had was finding enough arms for all of their soldiers. By the spring of 1776, under the command of General Charles Lee, Virginia could field an impressive force fully capable of dealing with Lord Dunmore.

Lord Dunmore established a base at Gwynn's Island south of the Rappahannock River, where he moved his fleet and continued raiding the countryside. On July 8, General Andrew Lewis arrived with a brigade of Virginians and began shelling the island and the ships. The British evacuated. On July 23, Lord Dunmore's fleet sailed up the Potomac River, destroying a mill along the Occoquan River before being driven off by the Prince William County militia. With his dwindling force now ravaged by smallpox, Lord Dunmore and his followers sailed for the British stronghold of New York in August. In the fall, Lord Dunmore returned to Britain. He continued to draw pay as Virginia's royal governor until 1783, when Britain recognized American independence.

INDEPENDENCE, 1776

The Fourth Virginia Convention convened in Williamsburg in December 1775, following Lord Dunmore's proclamation in November that the colony was in a state of rebellion. The convention declared that Virginians were ready to defend themselves "against every species of despotism." During the first four conventions, despite grumblings from radicals, no resolutions in favor of independence from the British empire were adopted. This was to dramatically change by the spring of 1776.

The Fifth Convention met in Williamsburg on May 6. There were three power groups represented at the Fifth Convention. The more conservative group represented the wealthy planters. The second group was made up of the political philosophers George Mason, George Wythe, Thomas Jefferson and James Madison. The third group was mainly from western Virginia and included radicals, such as Patrick Henry, who had supported independence earlier than 1775.

On May 15, the convention declared that the government of Virginia as "formerly exercised" by King George in Parliament was "totally dissolved." On June 7, Richard Henry Lee, one of Virginia's delegates to the Continental Congress, following the instructions of the Virginia Convention, proposed that "these United Colonies are, and of right ought to be, free and independent States, that they are absolved from all allegiance to the British crown, and that all political connection between them and the State of Great Britain is, and ought to be totally dissolved." While the Continental Congress debated Richard Henry Lee's proposal, the Virginia Convention adopted George Mason's "Virginia Declaration of Rights":

A DECLARATION OF RIGHTS made by the representatives of the good people of Virginia, assembled in full and free convention which rights do pertain to them and their posterity, as the basis and foundation of government.

Section 1. That all men are by nature equally free and independent and have certain inherent rights, of which, when they enter into a state of society, they cannot, by any compact, deprive or divest their posterity; namely, the enjoyment of life and liberty, with the means of acquiring and possessing property, and pursuing and obtaining happiness and safety.

Section 2. That all power is vested in, and consequently derived from, the people; that magistrates are their trustees and servants and at all times amenable to them.

Section 3. That government is, or ought to be, instituted for the common benefit, protection, and security of the people, nation, or community; of all the various modes and forms of government, that is best which is capable of producing the greatest degree of happiness and safety and is most effectually secured against the danger of maladministration. And that, when any government shall be found inadequate or contrary to these purposes, a majority of the community has an indubitable, inalienable, and indefeasible right to reform, alter, or abolish it, in such manner as shall be judged most conducive to the public weal.

Section 4. None of mankind is entitled to exclusive or separate emoluments or privileges from the community, but in consideration of public services;

which, not being descendible, neither ought the offices of magistrate, legislator, or judge to be hereditary.

Section 5. That the legislative and executive powers of the state should be separate and distinct from the judiciary; and that the members of the two first may be restrained from oppression, by feeling and participating the burdens of the people, they should, at fixed periods, be reduced to a private station, return into that body from which they were originally taken, and the vacancies be supplied by frequent, certain, and regular elections, in which all, or any part, of the former members, to be again eligible, or ineligible, as the laws shall direct.

Section 6. That elections of members to serve as representatives of the people, in assembly ought to be free; and that all men, having sufficient evidence of permanent common interest with, and attachment to, the community, have the right of suffrage and cannot be taxed or deprived of their property for public uses without their own consent or that of their representatives so elected, nor bound by any law to which they have not, in like manner, assented for the public good.

Section 7. That all power of suspending laws, or the execution of laws, by any authority, without consent of the representatives of the people, is injurious to their rights and ought not to be exercised.

Section 8. That in all capital or criminal prosecutions a man has a right to demand the cause and nature of his accusation, to be confronted with the accusers and witnesses, to call for evidence in his favor, and to a speedy trial by an impartial jury of twelve men of his vicinage, without whose unanimous consent he cannot be found guilty; nor can he be compelled to give evidence against himself; that no man be deprived of his liberty except by the law of the land or the judgment of his peers.

Section 9. That excessive bail ought not to be required, nor excessive fines imposed, nor cruel and unusual punishments inflicted.

Section 10. That general warrants, whereby an officer or messenger may be commanded to search suspected places without evidence of a fact committed, or to seize any person or persons not named, or whose offense is not particularly described and supported by evidence, are grievous and oppressive and ought not to be granted.

Section 11. That in controversies respecting property, and in suits between man and man, the ancient trial by jury is preferable to any other and ought to be held sacred.

Section 12. That the freedom of the press is one of the great bulwarks of liberty, and can never be restrained but by despotic governments.

Section 13. That a well-regulated militia, composed of the body of the people, trained to arms, is the proper, natural, and safe defense of a free state; that standing armies, in time of peace, should be avoided as dangerous to liberty; and that in all cases the military should be under strict subordination to, and governed by, the civil power.

Section 14. That the people have a right to uniform government; and, therefore, that no government separate from or independent of the government of Virginia ought to be erected or established within the limits thereof.

Section 15. That no free government, or the blessings of liberty, can be preserved to any people but by a firm adherence to justice, moderation, temperance, frugality, and virtue and by frequent recurrence to fundamental principles.

Section 16. That religion, or the duty which we owe to our Creator, and the manner of discharging it, can be directed only by reason and conviction, not by force or violence; and therefore all men are equally entitled to the free exercise of religion, according to the dictates of conscience; and that it is the mutual duty of all to practise Christian forbearance, love, and charity toward each other.

On June 29, the Fifth Convention approved the first Constitution of Virginia and chose Patrick Henry as the first governor of the Commonwealth of Virginia.

The ideas and language adopted by the Fifth Virginia Convention had far-reaching and enduring influence. The Continental Congress adopted Richard Henry Lee's proposal and appointed a committee of five to draft a declaration of independence. The lanky, ginger-haired Thomas Jefferson of Virginia wrote the first draft, which was then submitted to the full committee for revisions. The formal Declaration of Independence was approved on July 4, 1776.

THE HARD HAND OF WAR, 1776–1781

After the expulsion of Lord Dunmore's forces, Virginia was relatively peaceful for the next three years, although it sent forces to its frontier in the northwest, which then included much of the Ohio Country, a loosely defined region west of the Appalachian Mountains and south of Lake Erie. Several colonies made claims on parts of the region. Virginia claimed the entire region. The Shawnee and other Native American tribes in the Ohio Country allied with the British, hoping to expel the Virginians permanently from the Ohio Country. In 1778, Virginia's George Rogers Clark won victories at Fort Kaskaskia (in modern-day Illinois) and at the Battle of Vincennes (in modern-day Indiana). The Virginia legislature organized the newly conquered territories into Illinois County, Virginia.

The British brought the war back to coastal Virginia on May 8, 1779, when a fleet consisting of six warships, numerous Loyalist privateers and transports carrying 1,800 troops swept into Chesapeake Bay. This combined force had been sent from New York to disrupt the flow of Virginia supplies and troops going north to General Washington and south to General Benjamin Lincoln in South Carolina. Admiral George Collier landed troops at Hampton Roads and established Portsmouth as his base of operations. The British land commander, General Edward Mathew, demonstrating disdain for Virginia's land forces, sent out parties to raid. The Virginia militia began to turn out in force, but many were unarmed. Available muskets had been drained away by Virginia troops marching to other theaters of war. On May 24, as planned, the British ended their raid, having disrupted the flow of Patriot reinforcements and destroyed large quantities of food, gunpowder and naval stores.

On April 18, 1780, Thomas Jefferson, who had succeeded Patrick Henry as governor, moved the state capital from Williamsburg to Richmond, believing it safer from attacks by the British. The British came again in late October. British General Alexander Leslie entered Chesapeake Bay with 2,500 troops and established Portsmouth as a base of operations.

LE GENERAL ARNOLD un des Chefs
de l'Armée Anglo Americaine.

A Paris chez Esnauts et Rapilly, rue St. Jacques, a la Ville de Coutances: A.P.D.R.

The traitor Benedict Arnold, who had been made a British brigadier general, ordered the burning of Richmond. *Courtesy of the Library of Congress.*

Originally, Leslie intended to march on Richmond and Petersburg, but his raid ended on November 9 when he was ordered to reinforce General Cornwallis in the Carolinas.

The British returned in January 1781. A force of some 1,600 regular and Loyalist troops under the command of the traitor Benedict Arnold, who had been made a British brigadier general, sailed up the James River. They landed at Westover Plantation on January 4, 1781, remained here for about one week and then marched on Richmond.

Richmond (with a population of 1,800) was defended by several hundred militiamen, who showed little desire to face the British. After firing one volley at the oncoming British, the militia broke and ran. Arnold marched triumphantly into the town. Arnold wrote to Governor Thomas Jefferson, offering to spare Richmond if he was allowed to carry away the valuable bales of tobacco that had been found without hindrance. Jefferson refused to bargain. An enraged General Arnold ordered the town burned. He went on to destroy the Westham cannon foundry and burn homes across the James River in Chesterfield County.

The colonel of the Virginia militia, Sampson Mathews, put together a force of several hundred and began to pursue General Arnold's forces, engaging in a series of hit-and-run skirmishes. Arnold's army moved down the James River while being harried by Mathews. On January 19, Benedict Arnold's troops reached Portsmouth. In late March, General William Phillips arrived in Portsmouth with two thousand troops. Phillips, now in overall command of British forces in Virginia, took Petersburg on April 25. Phillips then moved toward Richmond, with the intention of gathering support from Loyalists and hampering Virginia's ability to aid Patriot forces in the Carolinas. He was prevented from seizing Richmond by the arrival of the Marquis de Lafayette with a sizeable number of troops. On May 13, Phillips died in Petersburg from fever. One week later, Major General Charles Lord Cornwallis arrived in Virginia, marching his army out of the Carolinas. Cornwallis was in command of more than seven thousand troops.

Cornwallis's forces raided as far west as Charlottesville and captured the main American supply depot at Point of Fork on the James River. Lafayette, now reinforced with Pennsylvania Continental Line troops under Brigadier General "Mad" Anthony Wayne and Virginia militia under Major General Baron Friedrich Von Steuben, had a force about half the size of that of Cornwallis and began to shadow the British, being careful not to bring on a general engagement.

Using tactics of slash and run, the Americans began to wear the British down. Lafayette remained unconquered. *Courtesy of the Library of Congress.*

In mid-June, Cornwallis turned toward the coast. Following a skirmish at Spencer's Ordinary west of Williamsburg on June 26, Cornwallis made plans to move his army across the James River at Jamestown and move on to Portsmouth. At this point, the canny general set a trap for Lafayette's army. Cornwallis leaked false plans indicating that now only a small rear guard was stationed near Jamestown. On July 6, Lafayette saw an opportunity to attack what he believed to be the vulnerable British rear guard.

Lafayette sent General Wayne and his corps to seize the opportunity. Before fully recognizing his position, General Wayne found himself engaged with the bulk of the British army in what is known as the Battle of Green Spring. Lafayette sent in reinforcements to support Wayne just as the British were about to outflank his line. Wayne concluded that retreat at this point would be disastrous and so ordered an assault, the ferocity of which checked the British advance, giving the Patriot forces an opportunity to escape. The British remained in possession of the battlefield, and Lafayette's forces moved away from the area that night.

The British now moved on to Portsmouth unhindered. Here the army was loaded onto troop transports. Lafayette believed that Cornwallis was headed for the British stronghold at New York City and was surprised to learn in early August that Cornwallis had landed at Yorktown and was fortifying both Yorktown and Gloucester Point on the opposite shore of the York River. On August 21, Lafayette wrote to General Washington of the possibility of taking on Cornwallis at Yorktown. Unknown to Lafayette, the Allied armies of America and France were already on their way to Yorktown.

VICTORY AT YORKTOWN, 1781

By the summer of 1781, the British believed that final victory depended on subduing Virginia. Virginia was the largest, wealthiest and most populated colony. It had provided men and supplies to rebel forces in both the Carolinas and in the North. Lord Cornwallis had been ordered to provide a protected harbor for the British fleet in the lower Chesapeake Bay. Cornwallis chose Yorktown because of its deep-water harbor on the York River. The British navy had long been unhappy with its naval base at New York City because of sandbars at the mouth of the Hudson River and winter freezes on the river that imprisoned ships.

Meanwhile, the Americans were making plans of their own. In the spring of 1781, General Washington traveled to Rhode Island to meet with his ally, the French commander the Comte de Rochambeau. A French fleet was expected to arrive in New York that summer; Washington and Rochambeau worked out a plan to attack the British in New York at the time of the fleet's arrival. Rochambeau's army marched to join Washington's troops outside New York City, only to learn on August 14 that the French fleet, commanded by Admiral de Grasse, was headed to the lower Chesapeake Bay.

A new plan was devised to attack Cornwallis in Virginia, while deceiving the British about the intentions of the Allied army. Washington prepared false plans, which he let fall into British hands, outlining the strategy for attacking New York City. Leaving a small force behind, Washington and Rochambeau moved south on August 19 to confront Lord Cornwallis.

Central to the new plan was the ability of the French fleet to gain control of the Chesapeake Bay and cut off British forces in Yorktown from being reinforced. On August 29, the French fleet anchored off Jamestown and

About 19,000 American and French soldiers were ready to face the 8,300 British and Hessian soldiers occupying Yorktown. *Courtesy of the Library of Congress.*

disembarked three thousand French troops. Now aware of the whereabouts of the French fleet, a British fleet reached the mouth of the Chesapeake Bay on September 5, 1781. The two fleets began to maneuver into battle position for the almost three-hour engagement known as the Battle of the Capes. The battle was a tactical French victory, with two French ships being damaged compared to six British ships. The fleets disengaged to assess damage but stayed within view of each other.

Unfortunately for the British, a fresh French fleet under Admiral de Barras, sailing down from Rhode Island, now appeared in the bay. Significantly outnumbered, the British fleet sailed for New York to make repairs, await the arrival of fresh ships and prepare to embark thousands of troops to reinforce Lord Cornwallis at Yorktown.

On September 14, Cornwallis received a letter assuring him that he would be reinforced. Despite the advice of Banastre Tarleton that Cornwallis should immediately try to fight his way out against the still comparatively weak army of Lafayette, Cornwallis decided to remain at Yorktown and await the reinforcements.

Reinforcements were indeed at hand, but they were reinforcements for the American side: Washington and Rochambeau had arrived. By the end of September, approximately 19,000 American and French soldiers (7,800 Frenchmen, 3,100 militia and 8,000 Continentals) were gathered at Williamsburg ready to face the 8,300 British and Hessian soldiers occupying Yorktown. Cornwallis received assurances that a British fleet with 5,000 men would sail for Yorktown from New York on October 5. The reinforcements could arrive as early as October 15. This was going to be a close-run thing.

Washington, Rochambeau and Admiral de Grasse held a council of war aboard the admiral's flagship. Admiral de Grasse agreed to provide marines and cannons and to delay his departure until the end of October. Rumors that British naval reinforcements had reached New York made Admiral de Grasse uneasy, and it took the persuasive talents of both Washington and Rochambeau to convince him to stay. Controlling the Chesapeake was essential if Cornwallis was to be bagged.

The British line of defense around Yorktown consisted of ten small enclosed forts (called redoubts) and batteries with light field artillery, all connected by manned trenches. The Americans and French began digging their own trenches eight hundred yards from the British line on September 28. By October 9, the allies were finished digging and had moved up their heavy siege artillery. During the next days, fifty heavy artillery pieces (including twenty-four-pounders, eighteen-pounders, howitzers and mortars) bombarded Yorktown. The French opened fire at 3:00 p.m. on October 9, with the Americans following at 5:00 p.m. General Washington fired the first American gun.

The Allied bombardment was devastating. American Captain James Duncan wrote:

> *The whole night was nothing but one continual roar of cannon, mixed with the bursting of shells and rumbling of houses torn to pieces. As soon as day approached the enemy withdrew their* [artillery] *pieces…and retired under cover of their* [earth] *works, and now commenced a still more dreadful cannonade from all our batteries without scarcely any intermission for the whole day.*

Inside the British lines, Lieutenant Bartholomew James wrote:

> *Upwards of a thousand shells were thrown into the works on this night* [October 11] *and every spot became alike dangerous. The noise and thundering of the cannon, the distressing cries of the wounded and the lamentable sufferings of the inhabitants, whose dwellings were chiefly in flames…must inevitably fill every mind with pity and compassion.*

Firing at the British continuously, the allies had virtually knocked the light British field artillery out of action by October 11. Cornwallis had the additional misfortune of learning that the departure of the promised reinforcements from New York had been delayed.

The allies began a second trench line even closer to the British. The new line could not be completed, however, without capturing the last major remaining British outer defenses, Redoubts 9 and 10. On the night of October 14, these redoubts were successfully stormed. The noose was tightening. On October 16, the British launched a desperate attack against the Allied center. This was repulsed. That night, the British tried to evacuate Yorktown by crossing the York River in small boats to Gloucester Point. A violent storm scattered the boats, making an evacuation impossible.

With his ammunition and provisions nearly exhausted, and at the mercy of the unrelenting heavy siege artillery, Lord Cornwallis was ready to talk surrender. On October 17, a British drummer followed by a British officer with a white flag brought a note requesting a ceasefire. On October 18, one American officer, one French officer and two British officers met at the Moore House, outside Yorktown, to settle surrender terms.

The British asked that their army be allowed to march out with flags flying, bayonets fixed and the band playing an American or French tune in tribute to the victors. General Washington refused such honors of war because the British had denied the defeated American army these honors after the surrender of Charlestown (as Charleston was spelled at the time), South Carolina. The British and Hessian troops marched to the surrender field with flags furled and muskets shouldered. Legend has it that the British band played "The World Turned Upside Down."

Lord Cornwallis was not present at the surrender due to alleged ill health. He was represented by Brigadier General Charles O'Hara. O'Hara first tried to offer the sword of surrender to the French, but General Rochambeau pointed to Washington. O'Hara offered his sword to Washington, but

Washington, affronted by the absence of Lord Cornwallis, had his second-in-command accept the sword.

And what about the reinforcements that might have saved Cornwallis? Bad weather and slow repairs delayed the departure of the fleet. It finally sailed from New York on October 19 and arrived off Yorktown on October 29, ten days too late to be of any help.

George Washington did not think that Yorktown would be the last battle of the Revolutionary War and felt that it was his duty to keep the Continental army together until a final peace treaty was signed. Despite the devastating loss at Yorktown, Loyalist militias continued to fight throughout the back country.

Peace talks began in April 1782. A preliminary treaty finally came on November 30, 1782, more than a year after Yorktown. The final treaty was signed on September 3, 1783, and was ratified by the Continental Congress early in 1784.

PART II

REVOLUTIONARY WAR SITES
YOU CAN VISIT

The following list, although not exhaustive, includes sites in Virginia that have an important connection to the major events and figures in the period of the American Revolution.

ABINGDON—ABINGDON MUSTER GROUNDS
This nine-acre site highlights the American Revolution in southwest Virginia. The muster grounds mark the northern trailhead of the 330-mile Overmountain Victory Trail used by Patriot militia during the Kings Mountain (South Carolina) campaign of 1780. The Battle of Kings Mountain pitted Patriot and Loyalist militias against each other in what has been called "the war's largest all-American fight."

The Keller Interpretive Center shows what life was like for the people of Abingdon and southwest Virginia.

ALBEMARLE COUNTY—MONTICELLO
This was the home of Thomas Jefferson. In 1776, Jefferson was chosen to draft the Declaration of Independence, putting forward the arguments of the colonies for declaring themselves free and independent states.

The Declaration is regarded as a charter of universal liberties, proclaiming that all men are equal in rights regardless of birth, wealth or status; that those rights are inherent in each human, a gift of the Creator, not a gift of government, and that government is the servant and not the master of the people.

The British had the opportunity to burn Monticello to the ground but, uncharacteristically, did not proceed with it. *Courtesy of the Library of Congress.*

Although slavery, practiced in all thirteen colonies at the time, made a mockery of Jefferson's poetic vision, no less a figure than Abraham Lincoln, the Great Emancipator, wrote:

> *All honor to Jefferson—to the man who, in the concrete pressure of a struggle for national independence by a single people, had the coolness, forecast, and capacity to introduce into a merely revolutionary document, an abstract truth, and so to embalm it there, that to-day and in all coming days, it shall be a rebuke and a stumbling-block to the very harbingers of reappearing tyranny and oppression.*

Jefferson left the Continental Congress in 1776, returning to Virginia as a member of the House of Delegates. In late 1776, he worked closely with James Madison in formulating the language and ideas that would become the Virginia Statute of Religious Freedom (1786), which disestablished the Church of England in Virginia and guaranteed freedom of religion to people of all religious faiths. This statute was to inspire the language in the First Amendment of the U.S. Constitution.

In 1781, Jefferson narrowly avoided being captured or killed by the British during a lightning raid on Monticello and nearby Charlottesville by the savage cavalry of Banastre Tarleton. Tarleton was known for using the style of *rage militaire* while conducting his campaigns. While a detachment sent to the house by Tarleton had the opportunity to burn Monticello to the ground, legend says that the British were so greatly impressed by the building that they uncharacteristically did not proceed.

Elected governor from 1779 to 1781, Jefferson was subjected to an inquiry into his alleged lax response to the 1781 British invasion of Virginia. Although found without fault, the harsh criticism he received left Jefferson with a lifelong bitterness toward Patrick Henry, his chief accuser. Jefferson said that the investigation "inflicted a wound on my spirit which will only be cured by the all-healing grave."

ALEXANDRIA—CHRIST CHURCH

The church building was completed in 1773 and became a center for pro-Revolutionary activity because the rector was particularly in favor of independence. The Revolution ended government financial support for the church, but Christ Church survived because of the support of prominent parishioners such as George Washington. Washington maintained a box family pew and attended services when in Alexandria.

ALEXANDRIA—THE OLD PRESBYTERIAN MEETING HOUSE

The original meeting house, erected in 1775, was largely destroyed by fire in 1835. The structure was rebuilt on the same site, with parts of the original walls. Forty-three Revolutionary War Patriots are buried in the churchyard burial ground and nearby Presbyterian Cemetery.

Dr. James Craik, surgeon general of the Continental army, is buried on the grounds of the meeting house. Dr. Craik served by George Washington's side at every battle until the British surrender at Yorktown. Dr. Craik dressed the wounds of General Lafayette at the Battle of Brandywine and tended to the dying General Hugh Mercer at the Battle of Princeton. After the war, Dr. Craik became Washington's personal physician and was present when Washington died at Mount Vernon.

Most of the graves at the Old Presbyterian Meeting House in Alexandria date to the eighteenth century, and most of those buried here were either personal friends of George Washington or known to him. The most unusual grave here is the Tomb of the Unknown Revolutionary War Soldier. In 1826, workers digging a foundation behind the Old Presbyterian Meeting House

"Here lies a soldier of the Revolution whose identity is known but to God." *Author's collection.*

found an unmarked grave, with an ammunition box serving as a coffin. The tattered uniform of the grave's occupant identified him as a Revolutionary War soldier, and the buttons on the uniform indicated that he was from Kentucky. The soldier's remains were reinterred at the cemetery behind the meeting house. In 1929, a memorial was created. An inscription placed on the table tomb at the dedication of the memorial reads:

> *Here lies a soldier of the Revolution whose identity is known but to God.*
> *His was an idealism that recognized a Supreme Being, that planted religious liberty*
> *on our shores, that overthrew despotism, that established a people's government,*
> *that wrote a Constitution setting metes and bounds of delegated authority,*
> *that fixed a standard of value upon men above gold and lifted*
> *high the torch of civil liberty along the pathway of mankind.*
> *In ourselves this soul exists as part of ours, his memory's mansion.*

ALEXANDRIA—CARLYLE HOUSE

In 1749, John Carlyle became one of the founding fathers of Alexandria. In 1753, the wealthy merchant built a grand home in Alexandria, overlooking the Potomac River. The magnificent stone house became a center of social and political activity. In 1774, Carlyle became a member of the Fairfax County Committee of Safety. He also signed the Fairfax Resolves in 1774. In October 1775, a visiting Englishman named Nicholas Cresswell portrayed the people of Alexandria as cursing the king and all things English and being "ripe for a revolt." Risking everything, John Carlyle warmly supported the Revolution when it came.

John Carlyle died in September 1780 at the age of sixty during the darkest days of the war. He is buried at the cemetery of the Old Presbyterian Meeting House in Alexandria.

ALEXANDRIA—GADSBY'S TAVERN

The first public celebration of Washington's birthday was at Valley Forge during the winter of 1778 on February 22. In Alexandria, the first was in 1780, yet Washington did not attend such a celebration in Alexandria until the Birth-night Balls at John Gadsby's City Tavern in 1798 and 1799. The City of Alexandria hosts the nation's oldest and largest George Washington Birthday Parade annually.

AUGUSTA COUNTY—AUGUSTA STONE PRESBYTERIAN CHURCH

The stone church has been in continuous use since 1749, making it the oldest Presbyterian church in continuous use in Virginia. The stone church in Augusta County served as both a meeting house and a frontier fort. The Founders Cemetery contains the graves of many Revolutionary War soldiers.

CHARLES CITY COUNTY—BERKELEY

Benjamin Harrison V was born in 1726 in this three-story Georgian brick mansion built by his father. Benjamin attended William and Mary College, but his education was cut short after a lightning strike killed his father and one of his sisters in 1745. Nineteen-year-old Benjamin returned to Berkeley and took over managing the plantation. The plantation's tobacco was shipped to England and was the basis of the family's fortune.

Benjamin Harrison served in the Virginia House of Burgesses for twenty-five years. After the dissolution of the Burgesses in 1774, he was elected as a delegate to the First Continental Congress. He remained in Congress until 1778. On June 7, 1776, Benjamin Harrison was chosen to introduce fellow

Virginian Richard Henry Lee, whose resolution called for independence from England. He was also selected to read Thomas Jefferson's draft of the Declaration of Independence to the delegates on July 1. Benjamin Harrison V was one of the fifty-six signers of the Declaration of Independence. During the war, he served as an officer in the county militia, served as a member of the House of Delegates and was elected governor of Virginia in 1781.

CHARLES CITY COUNTY—WESTOVER PLANTATION

At the time of the Revolution, this was the home of William Byrd III. Byrd inherited a large fortune, which he turned into a very small fortune through his lavish lifestyle and addiction to gambling. On July 6, 1774, Byrd made his will, disposing of an estate that "thro' my own folly and inattention to accounts the carelessness of some entrusted with the management thereof and the villainy of others, is still greatly encumbered with debts which embitters every moment of my life."

Byrd deplored the "frantic patriotism" sweeping Virginia and urged moderation and continued loyalty to the king. On July 30, 1775, he wrote offering his service to the king. In November 1775, however, he changed his mind after Lord Dunmore, the royal governor of Virginia, offered freedom to slaves who ran away and joined the fight against the Virginia revolutionaries.

This was too much for Byrd, who now sought appointment as colonel of the Third Virginia Regiment. This came to nothing, as did his attempt to persuade the Continental Congress to appoint him as a major general. In early January 1777, the embittered Byrd killed himself at Westover.

During Benedict Arnold's 1781 raid on Richmond, the British made Westover their base of operations for one week. William Byrd's widow, Mary Willing Byrd, was a cousin of Benedict Arnold's wife, Peggy Shippen.

CHARLOTTE COUNTY—THE GRAVE OF PATRICK HENRY

The grave of Patrick Henry is located at the family cemetery at Red Hill (Red Hill Patrick Henry National Memorial). He served as the first and sixth post-independence governor of Virginia and is best remembered for his "Give Me Liberty or Give Me Death" speech. Henry worked hard in the Patriot cause. As governor, he recruited the state's quota of six thousand men for the Continental army, as well as five thousand men for the Virginia militia. He supplied the Continental army with clothing and food, along with lead and gunpowder for ammunition. During his second term as Virginia governor, he supplied the George Rogers Clark Expedition, which conquered the Ohio Country.

CITY OF CHESAPEAKE—GREAT BRIDGE BATTLEFIELD & WATERWAYS MUSEUM
This museum interprets the Battle of Great Bridge in 1775, the first major Revolutionary War clash in Virginia. This "mini Bunker Hill" saw victorious Patriot militia maul British professional soldiers, sending them back to seek safety on their ships.

CITY OF FALLS CHURCH—FALLS CHURCH
The building was completed late in 1769. It is the oldest remaining church building in Virginia north of Quantico. During the Revolution, the church building was used as a recruiting station for the Fairfax County militia. Simon Sommers (1747–1836), a veteran of the Revolutionary War, is buried here. The Declaration of Independence was read to local citizens from the steps of the south doors.

COLONIAL WILLIAMSBURG—BRUTON PARISH CHURCH
The original part of the building was completed in 1715, with additions being made in 1721 and 1752. Because of its location in the colonial capital and because it was attended by the royal governor and other high officials, Bruton Parish Church was considered the "court church" of Virginia.

When they were members of the Virginia House of Burgesses, George Washington, Thomas Jefferson and Patrick Henry worshiped at Bruton when the legislature was in session. As part of a show of solidarity, members of the House of Burgesses marched in solemn procession to the church for a "Day of Fasting, Humiliation, and Prayer" in 1774 after the closing of the port of Boston.

The church's bell, the so-called Tarpley Bell (given by the wealthy merchant James Tarpley), was installed in the church tower in 1769. This bell is also known as "Virginia's Liberty Bell," not only because it was cast in the same foundry as the Liberty Bell in Philadelphia but also because it pealed out the good news in celebration of the Declaration of Independence.

COLONIAL WILLIAMSBURG—CAPITOL
At the time of the Revolution, the capitol was home to the Council of State and the House of Burgesses, the two houses of the Virginia General Assembly. Two buildings served Virginia on the same site: the first from 1705 until it was destroyed by fire in 1747 and the second from 1753 to 1780. The current building, reconstructed in the early 1930s, represents the first capitol.

It was in the capitol that Patrick Henry, George Washington, George Mason, Richard Henry Lee, Thomas Jefferson and other luminaries engaged in the debates leading up to the Revolution. The capitol at Williamsburg served until 1780, when Governor Thomas Jefferson moved the capital of Virginia to Richmond.

COLONIAL WILLIAMSBURG—THE GOVERNOR'S PALACE

In 1721, the Governor's Palace was completed. The impressive three-story structure would become home to nine governors of Virginia, including both Patrick Henry and Thomas Jefferson. In 1780, Thomas Jefferson moved the capital to its present location in Richmond. On December 21, 1781, the Governor's Palace, now being used as a hospital, burned to the ground, killing many soldiers recovering from wounds they sustained during the Yorktown campaign. The ruins of the Palace were covered over. The memory of the great structure would be lost until the 1930s, when the task of re-creating Colonial Williamsburg was undertaken. During the archaeological dig at the site, the remains of men crushed by the weight of the collapsing building were discovered.

On December 21, 1781, the Governor's Palace burned to the ground, killing many wounded soldiers inside. *Courtesy of the Library of Congress.*

COLONIAL WILLIAMSBURG—THE RALEIGH TAVERN

This was one of the largest taverns in colonial Virginia. It became famous as a gathering place for legislators after several royal governors officially dissolved the House of Burgesses. In May 1769, Governor Botetourt dissolved the House of Burgesses. The dismissed delegates immediately reconvened in the Apollo Room at the Raleigh Tavern and adopted the Non-Importation Agreement. The House of Burgesses was reconvened later that year by the governor.

Dissolved by Governor Dunmore in 1774, the Burgesses met once again in the Apollo Room in May 1774. The tavern was rebuilt in the 1930s.

COLONIAL WILLIAMSBURG—THE GEORGE WYTHE HOUSE

George Wythe was one of the most distinguished men in Virginia. Wythe was admitted to practice law before the bar of Virginia's General Court in 1746 at the age of twenty, becoming one of colonial Virginia's most preeminent lawyers. When Revolution came, Wythe was a member of the Continental Congress and signed the Declaration of Independence. After the Revolution, Wythe served as a judge and became the first professor of law at the College of William and Mary in Williamsburg. After the Revolution, taking the pronouncements of the Declaration of Independence seriously, Wythe began freeing his slaves and providing for their upkeep. Two freed slaves were living in Wythe's house: his housekeeper, Lydia Broadnax, and a free Black servant boy named Michael Brown. Wythe had made ample provision for both in his will.

The house served as George Washington's headquarters just before the Siege of Yorktown.

FAIRFAX COUNTY—GUNSTON HALL

Gunston Hall was the home of George Mason, a leading proponent of limiting the power of government and of protecting the rights of the people. Mason was the primary author of the Virginia Declaration of Rights and the Virginia Constitution, which greatly influenced the constitutions of other states. Thomas Jefferson incorporated many of Mason's ideas expressed in the Virginia Declaration of Rights into the Declaration of Independence.

George Mason served on the Fairfax County Committee of Safety, where he oversaw the creation of the Fairfax County militia. In April 1775, his remarks on annual elections for the company reflected his political philosophy on the eve of the Revolution:

We came equals into this world, and equals shall we go out of it. All men are by nature born equally free and independent. To protect the weaker from the injuries and insults of the stronger were societies first formed;…Every society, all government, and every kind of civil compact therefore, is or ought to be, calculated for the general good and safety of the community. Every power, every authority vested in particular men is, or ought to be, ultimately directed to this sole end; and whenever any power or authority whatever extends further, or is of longer duration than is in its nature necessary for these purposes, it may be called government, but it is in fact oppression.… In all our associations; in all our agreements let us never lose sight of this fundamental maxim–that all power was originally lodged in, and consequently is derived from, the people. We should wear it as a breastplate, and buckle it on as our armour.

Fairfax County—Mount Vernon

This was the home of George Washington. On June 15, 1775, the Continental Congress unanimously elected George Washington as the commander-in-chief of the Continental army. He was instructed to take immediate charge of the siege of Boston. George Washington wrote to his wife, Martha, at Mount Vernon to tell her of the change of circumstances: "I therefore beg, that you will summon your whole fortitude, and pass your time as agreeably as possible." Washington would not see his home for six years.

Martha Washington would spend half her time during those years traveling to the various camps of the Continental army to be with her husband. She spent the other half helping to manage Mount Vernon, with the able assistance of George Washington's third cousin Lund Washington. A building program, planned by George Washington before the war, was carried out, but the estate suffered from wartime shortages, a feared smallpox epidemic and threats from the British.

In April 1781, the British warship HMS *Savage* anchored off Mount Vernon. The British raiders took seventeen of Washington's slaves from the Mount Vernon plantation. Lund Washington went on board the *Savage*, took refreshments to the British officers and tried to negotiate the return of the enslaved people. He failed. One week later, Lafayette wrote to General Washington criticizing Lund's actions: "This being done by the gentleman who, in some measure, represents you at your house will certainly have a bad effect, and contrasts with spirited answers from some neighbors, that had their houses burnt accordingly." The general sent the

An officer found Mount Vernon an "elegant seat and situation, great appearance of opulence and real exhibitions of hospitality." *Courtesy of the Library of Congress.*

unfortunate Lund a stinging letter rebuking him for "communing with a parcel of plundering Scoundrels."

George Washington was to once again see Mount Vernon during his march to Yorktown in 1781. He arrived on the evening of September 9, along with one of his aides, Lieutenant Colonel David Humphreys, to a joyous welcome from Martha Washington, her son Jacky Custis and his wife and four small children, born while Washington was away at war.

During the course of the next two days, the rest of Washington's military aides plus two French generals and their ten aides arrived at Mount Vernon. Despite being a large group of visitors, they were all accommodated. One of Washington's aides found at Mount Vernon an "elegant seat and situation, great appearance of opulence and real exhibitions of hospitality and princely entertainment." Washington and his party left Mount Vernon at five o'clock in the morning on September 12, 1781.

Fairfax County—Pohick Church

Construction of this brick structure was completed in 1774 under the supervision of vestrymen George Washington and George Mason. A close friend of George Washington, Pohick's second rector, Reverend Lee Massey, wrote, "I never knew so constant an attendant at Church as [Washington]. And his behavior in the house of God was ever so deeply reverential that it produced the happiest effect on my congregation, and greatly assisted me in my pulpit labors. No company ever withheld him from Church. I have been at Mount Vernon on Sabbath morning when his breakfast table was filled with guests; but to him they furnished no pretext for neglecting his God and losing the satisfaction of setting a good example. For instead of staying at home, out of false complaisance to them, he used constantly to invite them to accompany him."

Two Revolutionary War soldiers, Peter Wagener and William Brown, are buried here.

Fredericksburg—Kenmore

Renamed Kenmore in 1819 by a later owner, this Georgian mansion was built in 1775 by wealthy merchant Fielding Lewis, the husband of George Washington's only sister, Betty. Fielding Lewis was a colonel in the Spotsylvania County militia. More importantly, he provided saltpeter, sulfur, powder and lead for the production of ammunition.

In 1775, Lewis was appointed with four others to establish and equip a manufactory of small arms for the newly formed Virginia government. Most of the operating capital for the new enterprise was provided by Fielding Lewis. By May 1777, the Fredericksburg Gunnery was producing twenty muskets, complete with bayonets, each week. Lewis also outfitted ships for the Virginia Navy, most notably the *Dragon*, which was built in Fredericksburg. The *Dragon* was initially used to protect the Rappahannock River from British and Loyalist raiders but was later used in the Chesapeake Bay.

Fielding Lewis's patriotic zeal ruined him financially, as he advanced increasingly large sums of money for the Patriot cause. Fielding Lewis died in December 1781, two months after the defeat of General Cornwallis at Yorktown.

Fredericksburg—Hugh Mercer Apothecary Shop

Hugh Mercer prospered as a respected doctor before the Revolution. Mercer was a member of the Fredericksburg Committee of Safety. In September 1775, he was elected colonel of the Minute Men of Spotsylvania, King

George, Stafford and Caroline Counties. On January 10, 1776, Mercer was appointed colonel of what was to become the Third Virginia Regiment of the Virginia Line. On June 5, 1776, he was made brigadier general in the Armies of the United Colonies. Mercer fought in the New York and New Jersey campaigns and was killed at the Battle of Princeton.

HANOVER COUNTY—SCOTCHTOWN

Patrick Henry, the great orator, lived here from 1771 to 1778. It was here he conceived his famous "Liberty or Death" speech. A native of Hanover County, Henry was primarily educated at home. He became a self-taught lawyer, opening a law practice in 1760. He was elected to the House of Burgesses, where he became known for his radical ideas and inflammatory rhetoric.

Patrick Henry's wife, Sarah, began to show signs of mental illness after the birth of her sixth child. *Courtesy of the Library of Congress.*

In 1774, Patrick Henry served as a delegate to the First Continental Congress. In 1776, he served on the committee charged with drafting the Virginia Declaration of Rights and the original Virginia Constitution. Patrick Henry was elected the first governor of post-independence Virginia and served from 1776 to 1779.

It is not generally known that during the time when he was becoming one of the leading Patriot leaders of Virginia, Patrick Henry was under severe pressure in his personal life. Henry's wife, Sarah, began to show signs of mental illness after the birth of her sixth child (some speculate that this was postpartum depression). Patrick Henry's mother wrote a letter in which she stated, "We feel Sarah is losing her mind after the birth of Neddy."

Sarah's doctor strongly recommended that she be sent to the new Eastern State Hospital in Williamsburg. Built in 1773, this was the only facility in Virginia at the time devoted to the care of the mentally ill. Patrick Henry refused to send his wife to the asylum and decided to keep her confined to the basement of the family home. This may actually have been a kindness, for although the new hospital was created with the best of intentions, the treatments were harsh. Patients were bled, blistered and subjected to pain, shock and terror. They were dunked in water and restrained.

Sarah's behavior was reputed to be unmanageable, and she was confined in a cellar room, bound in a straightjacket and attended by a servant. This secret was kept from the public. After several years of confinement, Sarah died in the spring of 1775 at the age of thirty-seven. She may have killed herself.

HANOVER COUNTY—HANOVER COURTHOUSE

Patrick Henry, then an obscure attorney, argued a case known as the "Parsons' Cause" at the Hanover Courthouse on November 5, 1763. This legal case is considered to be an important early defiance of royal authority.

According to Virginia legislation passed in 1748, Virginia's Anglican clergy (i.e., the established church's clergy) were to be paid annually in pounds of tobacco, the colony's primary cash crop. In 1758, the price of tobacco rose from two to six pennies per pound, thereby inflating clerical salaries. The House of Burgesses passed legislation (the "Two Penny Act") allowing what had previously been paid to the clergy as a set number of pounds of tobacco to be paid in currency at a rate of two pennies per pound, thus keeping clerical salaries at their traditional level. King George III vetoed the legislation.

James Maury sued in Hanover County Court in 1762 for back wages on behalf of all the local ministers who had been affected. Patrick Henry defended Hanover County against the claims, arguing that "a King, by disallowing Acts of this salutary nature…degenerated into a Tyrant and forfeits all right to his subjects' obedience."

The court ruled that Maury's claim was valid but that the amount of damages had to be determined by a jury. The jury awarded Maury one penny in damages. The award essentially nullified the king's veto, one of many defiant acts starting to manifest themselves.

LEXINGTON—THE GRAVE OF "LIGHT-HORSE HARRY" LEE

The grave is located in the University Chapel Museum. Because of his lightning mounted raids against the British, Lee earned the name "Light-Horse Harry." He joined Washington's army in 1776 and commanded a cavalry unit called "Lee's Legion" in 1778. He served in New Jersey and later served as a lieutenant colonel in the Southern theater under General Nathanael Greene. Lee wrote the famous eulogy for Washington's funeral, extolling George Washington as "first in war, first in peace, and first in the hearts of his countrymen."

He was the father of Civil War general Robert E. Lee.

LOUISA COUNTY—PROVIDENCE PRESBYTERIAN CHURCH

This two-story frame building was built in 1747. It is one of the few eighteenth-century frame churches still standing in Virginia. John Todd became Providence Church's first pastor in 1752. He remained in this position for more than forty years. Reverend Todd was an ardent supporter of the American Revolution and served as the chaplain of the Louisa County militia.

MADISON COUNTY—HEBRON EVANGELICAL LUTHERAN CHURCH

This is the oldest Lutheran church in Virginia. The central portion of the frame building was built in 1749 by German settlers. Prior to the Revolution, every person, regardless of denomination, was compelled to pay tithes to the Episcopal Church.

MATHEWS COUNTY—FORT CRICKET HILL REVOLUTION SITE

This earthwork fort, under the command of General Andrew Lewis, opened fire on the British on July 8, 1776, forcing Lord Dunmore to abandon Gwynn's Island and quit Virginia forever.

NORFOLK—ST. PAUL'S CHURCH

Formally known as the Borough Church and renamed St. Paul's in 1832, this is the only pre-Revolutionary building remaining in downtown Norfolk. In the early morning hours of January 1, 1776, the British fleet, in retaliation for Norfolk's refusal to supply provisions, opened fire on the town. A cannonball, fired from the British frigate HMS *Liverpool*, lodged in the church wall. Over the next two days, both British troops and Virginia and Carolina militiamen destroyed about two-thirds of the town. To prevent the British from occupying the town's strategic location, Colonel Robert Howe's colonial troops burned the remainder of the town on February 6. Only the walls of the Borough Church remained standing.

ORANGE COUNTY—MONTPELIER

This was the home of James Madison, the "Father of the U.S. Constitution" and fourth president of the United States. In 1774, Madison became a member of the local Committee of Safety, which oversaw the local militia. In October 1775, he was commissioned as a colonel of the Orange County militia. Madison never saw combat during the Revolutionary War, but he did rise to prominence in Virginia politics as a wartime leader and ally of Governor Thomas Jefferson.

James Madison was short, standing five feet, four inches tall and weighing in at about one hundred pounds. Madison was a sickly individual given to sudden seizures and attacks of "bilious fever." Madison's voice was so weak that people had difficulty hearing what he said. Despite his physical frailty, Madison was to serve two full terms as president of the United States. During the War of 1812, the sickly James Madison became the only sitting U.S. president to directly participate in a military action.

PETERSBURG—BLANDFORD CHURCH

The Blandford Church was erected in 1736 on the highest point in Petersburg. On April 25, 1781, one thousand militia under Major General Baron Von Steuben were defeated by some two thousand British regulars under the command of Brigadier General William Phillips. On May 13, the victorious Phillips fell ill with either typhus or malaria. As he lay dying in the home of the Bolling family, British forces in Petersburg were being bombarded by the cannons of the Marquis de Lafayette. After a shell hit the house and killed an African American servant named Molly, Phillips is reputed to have said, "Won't that boy let me die in peace?" Phillips died on May 13 and was secretly buried somewhere in the Blandford churchyard.

William Grayson was the first member of the U.S. Congress to die in office. *Courtesy of the Library of Congress.*

PRINCE WILLIAM COUNTY—THE TOMB OF COLONEL WILLIAM GRAYSON

At the outbreak of the American Revolution, William Grayson served as a captain of the local militia but left the Virginia forces to become an aide-de-camp to General Washington. He later took command of one of the sixteen regiments of the Continental army. After a bloody battle at Monmouth, New Jersey, that virtually destroyed his entire regiment, Grayson went on to serve on the Board of War. After the war, Grayson served as a member of the Continental Congress and was later one of Virginia's first two senators.

Grayson died in Dumfries on March 12, 1790, the first member of the U.S. Congress to die in office. He was interred at the Grayson family vault in Woodbridge on a hill overlooking Marumsco Creek. The family burial vault was originally located on a one-thousand-acre plantation. Now fewer than five acres remain undeveloped. The burial vault, now sitting in the midst of a Woodbridge residential neighborhood, was encased in concrete in the early 1900s by the Daughters of the American Revolution. Reverend Spence Grayson, a "fighting parson" of the Revolution and lifelong friend of George Washington, is also buried in the vault.

Prince William County—Rippon Lodge

This was the home of the Blackburn family, friends and neighbors of George Washington. Thomas Blackburn served in the House of Burgesses before the Revolution and served as a lieutenant colonel until severely wounded at the Battle of Germantown (Pennsylvania) in 1777.

On September 28, 1781, on its way to Yorktown, the American and French army's wagon train traveled south along the road "passing Blackburn House [Rippon Lodge] on the left."

Prince William County—Washington-Rochambeau Trail at Wolf Run Shoals

You can walk an original stretch of this famous trail at Wolf Run Shoals. In 1781, this was considered one of the best fords across the Occoquan River. George Washington ordered the Prince William County militia to improve the road from the ford in 1781. Shortly thereafter, French and American supplies passed this way during the march to Yorktown.

Richmond—Wilton

Originally known as World's End, this impressive house was built in 1753 for William Randolph III and his wife, Anne Carter Harrison Randolph, and commanded a two-thousand-acre tobacco and wheat plantation. In 1761, William Randolph III died, leaving the running of Wilton to his widow.

Anne Carter Harrison Randolph was active in the 1769 Association for the Non Importation of English Goods, one of the many ways Virginians initially expressed resistance toward Great Britain. In 1775, she provided hospitality to George Washington, who stayed at Wilton after attending the Second Virginia Convention and listening to Patrick Henry's stirring speech in favor of American independence. In 1781, the Marquis de Lafayette made Wilton his headquarters before marching to Yorktown with two thousand troops. Anne's young son served in the Continental army as an aide-de-camp to Lafayette.

The house was dismantled and moved to its current location in the twentieth century by the National Society of the Colonial Dames of America to save it from demolition.

Richmond—St. John's Church

The Second Virginia Convention was convened at St. John's Episcopal Church in Richmond on March 20, 1775. At this convention, Patrick Henry, a delegate from Hanover County, proposed raising a Virginia militia

William Wirt (1772–1834) reconstructed the accepted text of Patrick Henry's "Liberty or Death" speech for his biography of the orator. *Courtesy of the Library of Congress.*

independent of royal authority. His harsh language about the inevitability of war with Britain enraged moderates, sparking heated opposition. On March 23, Patrick Henry defended his proposal in one of the most historic and dramatic speeches in American history, which is presented in full here:

> *No man thinks more highly than I do of the patriotism, as well as abilities, of the very worthy gentlemen who have just addressed the House. But different men often see the same subject in different lights; and, therefore, I hope it will not be thought disrespectful to those gentlemen if, entertaining as I do opinions of a character very opposite to theirs, I shall speak forth my sentiments freely and without reserve. This is no time for ceremony. The questing before the House is one of awful moment to this country. For my*

own part, I consider it as nothing less than a question of freedom or slavery; and in proportion to the magnitude of the subject ought to be the freedom of the debate. It is only in this way that we can hope to arrive at truth, and fulfill the great responsibility which we hold to God and our country. Should I keep back my opinions at such a time, through fear of giving offense, I should consider myself as guilty of treason towards my country, and of an act of disloyalty toward the Majesty of Heaven, which I revere above all earthly kings.

Mr. President, it is natural to man to indulge in the illusions of hope. We are apt to shut our eyes against a painful truth, and listen to the song of that siren till she transforms us into beasts. Is this the part of wise men, engaged in a great and arduous struggle for liberty? Are we disposed to be of the number of those who, having eyes, see not, and, having ears, hear not, the things which so nearly concern their temporal salvation? For my part, whatever anguish of spirit it may cost, I am willing to know the whole truth; to know the worst, and to provide for it. I have but one lamp by which my feet are guided, and that is the lamp of experience. I know of no way of judging the future but by the past. And judging by the past, I wish to know what there has been in the conduct of the British ministry for the last ten years to justify those hopes with which gentlemen have been pleased to solace themselves and the House. Is it that insidious smile with which our petition has been lately received? Trust it not, sir; it will prove a snare to your feet. Suffer not yourselves to be betrayed with a kiss. Ask yourselves how this gracious reception of our petition comports with those warlike preparations which cover our waters and darken our land. Are fleets and armies necessary to a work of love and reconciliation? Have we shown ourselves so unwilling to be reconciled that force must be called in to win back our love? Let us not deceive ourselves, sir. These are the implements of war and subjugation; the last arguments to which kings resort. I ask gentlemen, sir, what means this martial array, if its purpose be not to force us to submission? Can gentlemen assign any other possible motive for it? Has Great Britain any enemy, in this quarter of the world, to call for all this accumulation of navies and armies? No, sir, she has none. They are meant for us: they can be meant for no other. They are sent over to bind and rivet upon us those chains which the British ministry have been so long forging. And what have we to oppose to them? Shall we try argument? Sir, we have been trying that for the last ten years. Have we anything new to offer upon the subject? Nothing. We have held the subject up in every light of which it is capable; but it has been all in vain. Shall we resort to entreaty and humble supplication? What terms shall we find which have not been already exhausted? Let us not, I beseech you, sir, deceive ourselves. Sir, we have done everything that could be done to avert the storm which is now coming on. We have petitioned; we have remonstrated; we have supplicated; we have prostrated ourselves before the throne, and have implored its interposition to arrest the tyrannical hands of the ministry and Parliament. Our petitions have been slighted; our remonstrances have produced additional violence and insult; our supplications have been disregarded; and we have been spurned, with contempt, from the foot of the throne! In vain, after these things, may we indulge the fond hope of peace and reconciliation? There is no longer any room for hope. If we wish to be free—if we mean to preserve inviolate those inestimable privileges for which we have been so long contending–if we mean not basely to abandon the noble struggle in which we have been so long engaged, and which we have pledged ourselves never to abandon until the glorious object of our contest shall be obtained–we must fight! I repeat it, sir, we must fight! An appeal to arms and to the God of hosts is all that is left us!

They tell us, sir that we are weak; unable to cope with so formidable an adversary. But when shall we be stronger? Will it be the next week, or the next year? Will it be when we are totally disarmed, and when a British guard shall be stationed in every house? Shall we gather strength by irresolution and inaction? Shall we acquire the means of effectual resistance by lying supinely on our backs and hugging the delusive phantom of hope, until our enemies shall have bound us hand and foot? Sir, we are not weak if we make a proper use of those means which the God of nature hath placed in our power. The millions of people, armed in the holy cause of liberty, and in such a country as that which we possess, are invincible by any force which our enemy can send against us. Besides, sir, we shall not fight our battles alone. There is a just God who presides over the destinies of nations, and who will raise up friends to fight our battles for us. The battle, sir, is not to the strong alone; it is to the vigilant, the active, the brave. Besides, sir, we have no election. If we were base enough to desire it, it is now too late to retire from the contest. There is no retreat but in submission and slavery! Our chains are forged! Their clanking may be heard on the plains of Boston! The war is inevitable–and let it come! I repeat it, sir, let it come.

It is in vain, sir, to extenuate the matter. Gentlemen may cry, Peace, Peace—but there is no peace. The war is actually begun! The next gale *that sweeps from the north will bring to our ears the clash of resounding arms! Our brethren are already in the field! Why stand we here idle? What is it that gentlemen wish? What would they have? Is life so dear, or peace so sweet, as to be purchased at the price of chains and slavery? Forbid it, Almighty God! I know not what course others may take; but as for me, give me liberty or give me death!*

William Wirt (1772–1834) reconstructed this accepted text of Patrick Henry's "Liberty or Death" speech for his biography of Patrick Henry.

Since 1976, St. John's Church Foundation has presented historical reenactments of the Second Virginia Convention of March 1775 at its original location. Professional actors portray nine delegates—including Patrick Henry, Thomas Jefferson and George Washington—who engage in the arguments of the Second Virginia Convention, leading to Patrick Henry's immortal speech. These reenactments are presented weekly during the summer months and on special patriotic holidays.

South Boston—Crossing of the Dan Exhibit

This exhibit explains the legendary "Race to the Dan," one of the most dramatic episodes of the war. In December 1780, the British army under Lord Cornwallis was on the verge of victory in the Southern theater of war. Cornwallis had captured Charlestown and had destroyed an American army at the Battle of Camden (South Carolina).

General Washington sent the able General Nathanael Greene to North Carolina to save the situation. Although outnumbered, Greene was both aggressive and smart, as he fought a guerrilla campaign against the British. On December 21, 1780, Greene sent General Daniel Morgan, a Virginian, into South Carolina with one wing of his army to harry the enemy. Morgan set a clever trap. He allowed the British under Lieutenant Colonel Banastre Tarleton to pursue his force until out of range of Cornwallis's main army. He then turned and decisively defeated Tarleton at the Battle of Cowpens. Morgan utterly smashed Tarleton's force and retreated north into North Carolina with huge numbers of prisoners as well as much-needed weapons and supplies.

General Greene reunited the two wings of his army in North Carolina as an enraged Lord Charles Cornwallis set out after the Americans with the bulk of his forces, intent on recapturing the prisoners taken by Daniel Morgan and smashing the Americans for good. Greene's objective now was to keep his smaller army out of the reach of the British. The Dan River was a significant natural barrier near the boundary of North Carolina and Virginia. If the Americans could reach the Dan, they could prevent the British from crossing. The "Race for the Dan" was on.

The Americans pushed the prisoners forward as rapidly as possible. The British burned their slow-moving supply wagons and pursued with remarkable speed, sometimes being only a few hours behind the Americans. Both sides were playing for high stakes.

On February 14, 1781, the American army reached Boyd's Ferry on the Dan River. Anticipating the arrival of General Greene's army, a flotilla of small boats had been assembled to carry men, supplies and cannons to safety. When the British arrived, they could only look with frustration at the impassable river.

The "Crossing of the Dan" exhibit is located at 700 Bruce Street in South Boston, on the site of the home of the Boyd family, the operators of the ferry where the American army crossed.

STAFFORD COUNTY—AQUIA CHURCH

Aquia Episcopal Church is the oldest active church in Stafford County. The current church was rebuilt in 1757. This was the childhood church of George Mason. Members of the parish were Patriot leaders of their day, including signers of the Leedstown Resolutions and an editor for the Virginia Statutes of Religious Freedom.

WESTMORELAND COUNTY—STRATFORD HALL

This was the hereditary seat of the Lee family, who boasted three brothers who were influential during the Revolution. Richard Henry Lee was a delegate to the Second Continental Congress, where he famously introduced the resolution for independence from Great Britain in 1776. He was one of the signers of the Declaration of Independence. He became one of post-independence Virginia's first two senators. His brother Francis Lightfoot Lee was also a delegate to the Continental Congress in 1776. Richard Henry and Francis Lee were the only two brothers to sign the Declaration of Independence. Another brother, Arthur Lee, was appointed by the Continental Congress as a commissioner to France to seek support for the Patriot cause.

WINCHESTER—THE GRAVE OF DANIEL MORGAN

Daniel Morgan is buried at the Mount Hebron Cemetery. Morgan left Pennsylvania as a young man and settled in Charles Town, Virginia, on the frontier. Morgan gained a reputation as a brawler. By 1774, he had become a prosperous farmer, owning 255 acres and ten slaves. In 1774, as a captain of militia, he fought against the Shawnee Indians in the Ohio Country. In 1775, the Continental Congress authorized the raising of ten rifle companies. Captain Daniel Morgan was selected to lead one of the companies. Morgan raised ninety-six men in ten days. Morgan's Grove Community Park near Shepherdstown, West Virginia (then part of Virginia), was the mustering point for Morgan's men. On July 15, Morgan and his company set out on the famous "Bee Line" march, marching six hundred miles in twenty-four days to join Washington's forces at Boston.

Morgan served in the expedition against Canada in 1775 and at the Battle of Saratoga in 1777. Morgan rejoined Washington's main army on November 18, skirmishing and scouting for Washington throughout New Jersey and Pennsylvania. Morgan offered his resignation from the army in 1779, dissatisfied with the Congressional policy on the promotion of officers. Congress refused his resignation and instead granted a furlough. He returned to active duty in September 1780 in the Southern theater. On October 13, 1780, Congress finally promoted Morgan to brigadier general. Morgan won a decisive victory over the British at the Battle of Cowpens (South Carolina) in 1781. The battle was the turning point of the war in the South.

Yorktown—American Revolution Museum at Yorktown
This world-class museum features period artifacts, immersive exhibits, holograms and dramatic films, including "The Siege of Yorktown," featuring a 180-degree surround screen and outstanding special effects.

Yorktown—Victory Monument
The cornerstone of this monument was laid on October 19, 1881, to mark the centennial of the surrender of the British at Yorktown. The monument to Alliance and Victory was completed on August 12, 1884. A figure of Liberty stood atop the monument. On July 29, 1942, during the darkest days of World War II, lightning struck the Liberty statue, shearing off the arms and head. The body was shattered and the base of the monument damaged. Some thought that this was an omen predicting the end of America. But America did not end, and after victory in World War II was achieved, the monument was restored to its former glory in 1956, spurred on by the efforts of the Sons of the American Revolution.

The monument to Alliance and Victory was completed on August 12, 1884. A figure of Liberty stood atop the monument. *Courtesy of the Library of Congress.*

YORKTOWN—BATTLEFIELD

Sixteen miles of the battlefield can be explored by car or on foot. Two historic buildings associated with the battle are the Moore House and the Nelson House. Negotiations for the British surrender occurred at the Moore House.

The Nelson House was home to Thomas Nelson Jr., a native of Yorktown. He was a wealthy merchant who was appointed colonel of the Second Virginia Infantry Regiment. In mid-1775, Nelson was elected to the Continental Congress and was one of the signers of the Declaration of Independence. In 1781, Nelson was elected governor of Virginia.

Nelson joined Washington and Rochambeau in besieging the British at Yorktown. As commander of the Virginia militia, Nelson was in charge of one-third of the American troops engaged in the siege. Nelson believed that British officers would be quartered in his fine mansion and supposedly paid to be the first artillerist to shell the house. Evidence of the artillery damage can still be seen.

The war ruined Nelson financially. His business never recovered, and the huge personal loans he made to help finance the war were never repaid. Nelson was left a poor man, in poor health, with a wife and eleven children. He died on the edge of poverty and was buried in an unmarked grave at Yorktown's Grace Church so that his creditors could not impound his body as collateral.

A man of true conviction, Nelson stated, "I would do it all over again," truly fulfilling the pledge that the signers of the Declaration Independence made on July 4, 1776:

> *…and for support of this Declaration, with a firm reliance*
> *on the protection of Divine Providence, we mutually*
> *pledge our lives, our fortunes, and our sacred honor.*

PART III

HOW THEY LIVED

Civilian Life

SLAVERY IN VIRGINIA

In the late summer of 1619, a storm-beaten Dutch ship (possibly a pirate ship) appeared in the harbor at Jamestown. The ship had nothing to trade except twenty Africans recently taken from a Spanish vessel. An exchange for food was made, and the Dutch ship sailed away. It is not clear if the Africans were considered slaves or indentured servants by the English settlers. There was no precedent in England for enslaving a class of people for life and making that status perpetual. It is clear, however, that by 1640, at least one African had been declared a slave. This African was ordered by the court "to serve his said master or his assigns for the time of his natural life here or elsewhere."

Although Black people were held in hereditary servitude long before Virginia laws specifically recognized slavery, a large number of Virginia's Black population worked as servants for a limited term or otherwise earned their freedom just like white indentured servants. White and Black servants worked together in the fields, sharing the same punishments, the same food and the same living quarters. The most remarkable evidence of a racially open society comes from the records of Northampton County. These records indicate that some 29 percent of the county's Black residents were free and that at least two of these, Francis Payne and Anthony Johnson, were planters (Johnson even becoming a slave owner himself).

During the second half of the seventeenth century, the British economy improved, and the supply of British indentured servants declined as poor Britons had better economic opportunities at home. To lure cheap labor to America, terms of indentures became fixed and shorter. By the 1670s, Virginia had a large number of restless and relatively poor white men (most of them former indentured servants) threatening the established order of the wealthy and propertied. A popular revolt in 1676, the so-called Bacon's Rebellion, led Virginia planters to begin importing Black slaves in large numbers in preference to the more expensive and politically restive white indentured servants.

The increasingly high price of free labor was incompatible with the profitable running of tobacco plantations. The landowners turned to slave labor, encouraging the first massive introduction of enslaved people from Africa in 1698. The new labor force was more controllable because Black people, as a group, were not normally thought to be naturally guaranteed the "rights of Englishmen" accorded to white freemen. In short, the system was to be based purely on force, and Virginia's laws soon reflected this.

The differences between Virginia's slave codes and the slave codes in the Spanish colonies of America were striking. Spain recognized the slave as a legal person. Virginia did not. As a legal person, the slave retained rights over which the master had absolutely no power. In Cuba, for example, a slave's family was protected by law. A master could not outrage a slave's wife or daughter. A slave had recourse to law and had a right to legal marriage. In Virginia's system of chattel slavery, an enslaved person had none of these rights. A slave was a thing, an economic commodity. Thus, in Virginia, the killing of a slave by a master was not a felony because, the law reasoned, "it cannot be presumed that prepensed malice should induce a man to destroy his own estate."

The need for long-term forcible control of a large enslaved population (some 40 percent of the population of Virginia by the late 1700s) was an unintended consequence of short-term decisions made for immediate economic gain.

The view of slavery in Great Britain itself was very different from that of the colonies. James Somerset was an enslaved man taken to England by his master, Charles Steuart, of Boston, Massachusetts. In 1771, while in England, Somerset escaped from his enslaver. He was recaptured and put in chains aboard the ship *Ann and Mary*, which was preparing to sail for Jamaica. Before the ship sailed, Somersett's godparents, supported by British abolitionists, applied to the Court of King's Bench for a writ of habeas corpus. The captain of the ship was required to produce Somersett so the court could decide if his imprisonment was legal. Lord Mansfield, the presiding judge, ordered Somersett to be released, finding that neither English common law nor any law made by Parliament recognized the existence of slavery in England. The Somersett case was a boon to the growing abolitionist movement in Great Britain and ended the holding of slaves in Britain. It did not end Britain's participation in the slave trade or end slavery in other parts of the British empire, such as the American colonies, all of which had positive laws allowing slavery.

In 1773, as the people of the American colonies railed against the Crown over matters of taxes, the General Court in Boston received the first of three petitions in which advocates for the enslaved argued that Lord Mansfield's decision should apply to the colonies since people were being "held in a state of Slavery within a free and Christian country." The issue of slavery was never to be decided in the colonial courts. Relations with the Crown continued to deteriorate leading to armed rebellion.

The dichotomy between the rhetoric of "liberty" and the reality of slavery in all of the restive thirteen colonies was not lost on either the enslaved or the

Most of the enslaved were field hands, although some were trained to be skilled craftsmen or household servants. *Courtesy of the Library of Congress.*

British. Loyal Britons questioned, "How is it that we hear the loudest yelps for liberty among the drivers of Negroes?"

At the time of the Revolution, slavery was an economic reality for white Virginia families, the rightness of which was never questioned. In the eighteenth century, Virginians' vision of slavery was based on the notion of benevolent paternalism, a system of mutual rights and responsibilities beneficial to both enslavers and enslaved. White Virginians wanted to believe that their slaves were basically happy, to the point that they would prefer to serve their enslavers rather than to choose their own freedom. White Virginians could never acknowledge that the "special relationship" between master and slave was not one of benign paternalism, parent to tutored child.

As the head of one prominent slave owning family later wrote, "The blacks are immeasurably better off here than in Africa, morally, physically, and socially. The painful discipline they are undergoing is necessary for their further instruction as a race, and will prepare them, I hope, for better things. How long their servitude may be necessary is known and ordered by a merciful Providence."

George Washington himself once explained to a foreign visitor that slavery was neither a crime nor an absurdity, noting, "Until the mind of the slave has been educated to understand freedom, the gift of freedom would only assure its abuse."

The relationship of enslavers to the enslaved was a straightforward business proposition: enslavers insisted on turning a profit from the enslaved. The pattern of life for the enslaved followed a pattern familiar throughout Virginia. The workday was from sunrise to sunset, with two hours off for meals. Sunday was a free day. Slaves received several days off at Christmas and the Mondays after Easter and Pentecost.

Most of the enslaved were field hands, although some were trained to be skilled craftsmen or household servants. The enslaved received a weekly food allowance, consisting of such staples as cornmeal and salted fish, which they supplemented by keeping their own gardens, fishing and hunting (in essence they subsidized their own enslavement in their free time). Slaves were issued clothes once per year. Male field hands wore coarse linen shirts, breeches, stockings and shoes without buckles. Women wore ankle-length dresses made of calico or linen. They also wore stockings and shoes without buckles.

Slave flight, "running away," the most common form of slave resistance, called into question the notion of benevolent paternalism and struck particularly hard at the idea that the enslaved were basically happy. Most running away was not permanent running. It might better be termed "absenteeism" and was a statement of resistance. Most slaves who sneaked away overnight or for a few days did so to avoid immediate punishment or to visit nearby wives, husbands or other family members. This absenteeism was so common that most masters dealt with it by inflicting only mild punishments. The more serious form of running away, which involved staying away from the plantation for weeks or months, was labeled "lying out." These runaways lived by fishing, hunting, stealing and trading. They camped near towns and cities, along rivers or in dense forests. They often formed small groups. Masters dealt with this type of behavior more harshly. White farmers throughout the South complained about Black runaways "lurking about near the plantations" and doing "mischief." Few runaways remained permanently at large; however, the Great Dismal Swamp between Virginia and North Carolina was home to large numbers of permanent runaways.

Many murders in Virginia revolved around the institution of slavery. There was born in colonial Virginia a relentless fear of slave uprisings that would last into the nineteenth century and significantly contribute to the coming of the Civil War because of the paranoiac siege mentality that it created. In 1774, William Pittman, a slaveholder in King George County, was accused of beating a slave to death in a drunken rage. Pittman testified that he was merely enforcing discipline over the slave for neglecting to take care of a horse and that he regretted the death. Enforcing discipline over unruly slaves was generally considered necessary and laudable. Pittman, however, was found guilty and sent to the gallows. Pittman's case was unusual in that most slaveholders were never brought to justice for the murder of an enslaved person (since the testimony of Black people was inadmissible evidence).

RELIGION

Freedom of religion, as we understand it, did not exist in Virginia until after the American Revolution. The Church of England was legally made the established church of Virginia in 1619. An Anglican parish contained a central church and two or more smaller chapels. Churches needed to be close enough for people to travel to the mandatory worship services. Civil penalties were attached to non-attendance. The spiritual leader of the parish was the rector, but the parish was governed by a committee of twelve leading laymen known as the vestry. The established church was closely linked to the political and financial elites. George Washington and George Mason, for example, were at times on the vestry of Pohick Church.

The vestry set the annual parish levy, one of the largest taxes paid by colonists. This tax provided for the minister's upkeep and provided for the destitute and disabled of the parish. Additionally, the vestry provided the priest with a church farm (known as a glebe) of two or three hundred acres, as well as a house. The vestry also appointed churchwardens, who were responsible for presenting moral offenders to the county courts. Vestrymen were required to swear allegiance to the laws of England and Virginia. Catholics were barred from serving, but prominent members of some of the so-called dissenting Protestant denominations served on vestries.

By the time of the Revolution, "dissenters," non-Anglican colonists who were predominantly Baptists or Presbyterians, made up a sizeable portion of the population. Although tolerated, dissenters were required to pay taxes to support the Anglican Church, in addition to paying for their own church and pastor. Dissenting pastors and their meeting houses had to receive licenses from the colony's General Court, which met twice a year in Williamsburg. Additionally, the law dictated that only ministers of the established church could legally perform baptisms, marriage ceremonies and funerals, which resulted in such anomalies as requiring a Lutheran minister to become an ordained minister of the Church of England in order to legally perform a marriage ceremony in his own church.

Some dissenters refused to comply with the law. Many believed that preaching need not be confined to the pulpit and that the state had no right to dictate where and to whom believers could preach the gospel. Evangelicals preaching to the enslaved (which would, it was thought, encourage revolt) was a major area of concern. Methodists and Baptists actively made conversions among the enslaved and free Blacks. Methodists encouraged an end to slavery. During the Revolutionary War, some seven hundred enslaved Methodists, including the congregation of an African American Methodist preacher named Moses Wilkinson, self-liberated by going behind British lines. The British transported these and many other Black Loyalists to Nova Scotia after the end of the war.

By the early 1770s, Baptists had become the fastest-growing denomination in Virginia. Fielding large numbers of itinerant self-proclaimed missionaries, the Baptists were drawing new followers, especially among poor white farmers and the enslaved. The Anglican Church struck back using the law, jailing Baptists guilty of illegal preaching. The first recorded imprisonment

Bruton Parish Church. Freedom of religion, as we understand it, did not exist in Virginia until after the Revolution. *Courtesy of the Library of Congress.*

of Baptists occurred in Spotsylvania County on June 4, 1768. Five unlicensed preachers were put on trial. The prosecutor proclaimed, "These men are great disturbers of the peace; they cannot meet a man upon the road, but they must ram a text of scripture down his throat."

In June 1776, the Virginia Convention adopted the Declaration of Rights, the sixteenth article of which proclaimed, "That religion, or the duty which we owe to our Creator and the manner of discharging it, can be directed by reason and conviction, not by force or violence; and therefore, all men are equally entitled to the free exercise of religion, according to the dictates of conscience; and that it is the mutual duty of all to practice Christian forbearance, love, and charity towards each other." Although this Declaration of Rights endorsed the concept of religious pluralism under the law, it was not until after the war, and the adoption of the Virginia Statute of Religious Freedom in 1786, that the established church was disestablished. The principle of protecting religious pluralism would subsequently be included in the First Amendment to the U.S. Constitution (1791).

HOW THEY TRAVELED

Movies often give the impression that everyone in the eighteenth century owned a horse. In fact, horses were transportation reserved for the upper class and professionals because of the expense involved in keeping them. At most, a horse could effectively cover about fifty miles per day, and most common folk walked if they needed to travel. In the colonial period, the Virginia gentry traveled often by horse and carriage to visit family and friends, to attend social events and to take part in the political life of Williamsburg. The circumference of travel was generally fairly small except for business or political reasons.

Overland on horseback from Williamsburg to Richmond (fifty miles), in good weather, would take one day. The journey from Williamsburg to Charlottesville could take four days and to the Shenandoah Valley five or more days. Even riding the fastest horse, a trip from Williamsburg to New York City would take ten days. The most famous overland trip from New York to Williamsburg was that made by the allied Franco-American army of George Washington and General Rochambeau. The army began its march on August 19, 1781, and arrived in Williamsburg, a march of some four hundred miles, on September 14.

The easiest method of travel between Williamsburg and Philadelphia or New York City was by ship. The trip to Philadelphia would take about a week and to New York ten to fourteen days, depending on the weather. Over land, the journey could take twice as long. Ships traveling across the Atlantic took at least six weeks.

During the Revolution, Martha Washington, to her everlasting credit, frequently visited her husband at the front. She joined her husband's Revolutionary army each winter for eight years, becoming famous for her warmth and loyalty. Even for Lady Washington, who had her own enclosed carriage, road travel in the eighteenth century was nasty, brutish and slow. Those vehicles that did venture out on the roads, most often slow-moving stagecoaches, were covered with mud or dust from top to wheel, rattled along uncomfortably, sometimes overturned and frequently sank into bogs. Large rivers were difficult to bridge. Ferries were used instead. The ferry was either a barge or a raft and was pulled across by workhorses or oxen on shore. Since they were skittish, horses were prone to cause accidents. George Washington recounted a typical road mishap: "In attempting to cross the ferry at Colchester with the four horses harnessed to the chariot…one of the leaders got overboard when the boat was in

Even for Lady Washington, who had a carriage, road travel in the eighteenth century was nasty, brutish and slow. *Courtesy of the Library of Congress.*

swimming water and fifty yards from the shore….His struggling frightened the [other horses] in such a manner that one after another and in quick succession they all got overboard…and with the utmost difficulty they were saved [and] the carriage escaped being dragged after them."

Early colonists used a network of paths made long before by Indians and wild animals to shape the earliest pattern of roads. The first turnpike in the country began construction in Virginia in 1785, running from Alexandria into the lower Shenandoah Valley. This wide, comfortable toll road spanned only thirty-four miles and took twenty-six years to complete, being completed in 1811. It was a marvel to travelers. In some cases, local governments built new roads, but more frequently private corporations were set up for the purpose; a profit of 20 percent earned from tolls was not uncommon. Notwithstanding these efforts, Virginia's roads had not improved much by the 1860s. No less a personage than General Robert E. Lee complained, "It has been raining a great deal…making the roads horrid and embarrassing our operations." Army wagons simply broke down on the roads because of the mud and rocks.

Family Life

In June 1734, the *South Carolina Gazette* printed a prayer for young ladies that called on "Virgin Powers" to defend them against "amorous looks" and "saucy love." When tempted to commit an indiscretion, respectable women should arm themselves with "honour" and "a guard of pride." Avoiding company and behavior that might compromise one's reputation did not require prudery or self-isolation. Conduct manuals appearing in the late eighteenth century advised young women to steer a middle course between undue familiarity, which was dangerous, and cold reserve, which made them undesirable. Smoothly engineered marriages among the wealthy required that children recognize suitable marriage partners, weeding out frauds, rakes and gold diggers. The successful transmission from parent to child of standards of quality, breeding and social position prevented children of the elite from straying too far from people of whom their parents approved.

Well-to-do families saw to it that their daughters acquired an education that included practical, literary and ornamental skills. These included cooking, sewing and household management; reading, writing and perhaps a little arithmetic and French; and a number of other niceties such as polished manners, musical training, dancing, drawing and fancy needlework.

Courting took place at organized functions such as dances, horse races and church. Dancing was an important courting ritual among the wealthy. It was considered a good way to determine a potential marriage partner's physical soundness, as well as the state of their teeth and breath. Dancing taught poise, grace and balance, especially important to women, who had to learn to remain in their "compass," or the area of movement allowed by their clothing. Balls often lasted three to four days and took all day and most of the night. They were the primary means of socializing in Virginia.

Women, then as now, had ways of making themselves more alluring. Among the elite, cosmetics were commonly worn. Almost everyone had a pockmarked face due to the widespread scourge of smallpox, but a handsomely pocked face was not considered unattractive, only an excessively pocked one. Flour, white lead, orrisroot and cornstarch were common bases to produce the aesthetic of a pure white face. Over these red rouge was used to highlight cheekbones, in a manner that would be considered exaggerated by modern standards but was most effective in the dim light afforded by candles in the eighteenth century. Lip color and rouge were made from crushed cochineal beetles. Cochineal was an expensive imported commodity; country women substituted berry stains. Carbon was used to highlight eyebrows and lashes, which were groomed with fine combs. The key aspects of the eighteenth-century cosmetic look were a complexion somewhere between white and pale, red cheeks and red lips. The ideal woman had a high forehead, plump rosy cheeks, pale skin and small lips, soft and red, with the lower lip being slightly larger, thus creating a rosebud effect. Although bathing one's entire body was not a regular occurrence in the eighteenth century, the daily washing of one's face and hands was a norm among the elite social circle.

An almanac essay titled *Love and Acquaintance with the Fair Sex* assures us that men were incapable of "resistance" against a woman's "attractive charms of an enchanting outside in the sprightly bloom of happy nature; against the graces of wit and politeness; against the lure of modesty and sweetness." Of course, some men felt uneasy about female allurements, which could account for the introduction of a bill before the British Parliament in 1770 titled "An Act to Protect Men from Being Beguiled into Marriage by False Adornments." The proposed act read, "All women, of whatever rank, age, profession or degree, whether virgins, maids or widows, that shall, from and after such Act, impose upon, seduce or betray into matrimony, any of His Majesty's subjects, by the use of scents, paints, cosmetic washes, artificial teeth, false hair, Spanish wool, iron stays, hoops, high-heeled shoes and bolstered hips, shall incur the penalty of the law in force against witchcraft and like misdemeanours and that the marriage upon conviction shall stand null and void."

The ideal woman according to "Advice to Unmarried Ladies," appearing in the *American Herald* in 1789, was demure and modest and avoided confrontation in conversation. Physical traits included "a pretty foot, good teeth, pretty hands and arms, and the finest voice." Depictions of women outside the elite were quite different. One essayist claimed that "not everyone" had "a mind capable of loving" and that "vulgar minds" in particular lacked the "organs" requisite for that exalted emotion; they experienced only lust. Poorer women were characterized as naturally lustful, whereas ladies were blessed with virtue and should take care not to lose it.

In upper- and middle-class families, a successful courtship concluded with the two fathers working out financial arrangements. These arrangements differed greatly depending on the wealth and position of the parents, but generally, the young man's parents were expected to be the most generous, providing land, a house, cattle and tools. The bride's parents contributed clothing, furniture, linens and money. When all financial arrangements were settled, the banns were read in a church, and the couple was officially considered to be engaged.

Martha was slightly younger than the average Virginia bride, who married at age twenty-two. *Courtesy of the Library of Congress.*

At the age of eighteen, Martha Dandridge stood about five feet tall, somewhat shorter than the average five feet, three inches of women of the day. By all accounts she was lovely with a lively personality, warm, dutiful, strong and sincere. She received the education typical of girls of her class. She met her first husband, Daniel Parke Custis, at their local Anglican church. Custis was the son of one of the wealthiest men in Virginia, John Custis IV, who owned thousands of acres of land, had almost three hundred slaves and sat on the Governor's Council in Williamsburg. Daniel Parke Custis was some twenty years older than Martha Dandridge. He lived on his own plantation, White House, situated four miles downstream from the Dandridge home on the Pamunkey River. When word of his son's interest in Martha surfaced, John Custis IV initially opposed the match. He insisted that the Dandridges lacked sufficient wealth and status to marry into his family and threatened to disinherit his son. Although Martha's father owned five hundred acres of land and fifteen to twenty slaves, he was not close to being among the wealthiest men in Virginia.

When Daniel pursued the match over his father's objections, family friends intervened with his father on their behalf. Martha arranged a meeting with Daniel's father, where she made her own case. The elder Custis concluded that Martha was "beautiful and sweet tempered" and gave his consent for the marriage. Martha Dandridge and Daniel Parke Custis married on May 15, 1750. Almost nineteen years old, Martha was slightly younger than the average Virginia bride, who married at age twenty-two. At thirty-eight, Daniel Parke Custis was nearly twenty years older than his new wife and significantly older than the average Virginia groom, who married for the first time at age twenty-seven. The marriage lasted seven years. Martha then found herself a widow and one of the wealthiest women in the colonies.

Martha did not remain a widow long, as suitors began to appear at her plantation, including a colonel of the Virginia militia, George Washington, a celebrated war hero of the war with the French and Indians. Washington sprang from the moderately prosperous Virginia gentry rather than one of the leading planter families. His background mirrored Martha's own. In March 1758, George visited Martha twice; the second time he came away greatly encouraged.

Charles Carter, a Virginia planter of far greater wealth and status than Colonel Washington, wrote to his brother about what a beauty she was and how he hoped to "arouse a flame in her breast." Carter failed, and Martha Dandridge Custis married George Washington on January 6, 1759. The couple honeymooned for several weeks before setting up housekeeping at Washington's Mount Vernon estate.

Virginia's colonial society placed the family, headed by a man, at the center of the social order. Families were defined as "little cells of righteousness" that held a watchful eye over the conduct of every individual and enforced the laws of God. Colonial society expected free white women to marry, to bear children and to manage a household in which they were economically productive but faithful, obedient and subordinate to men. A woman had a right to the love and support of her spouse but did not have a right to question his judgment.

Men were expected to marry, produce offspring, enjoy the companionship of a chosen wife and head an orderly household. Well into the eighteenth century, dominant marriage ideals stressed that love emerged over time, largely following, rather than preceding the wedding. The popular sermon "A Wedding Ring" reminded eighteenth-century Anglo-Americans that harmony was the foundation for a good marriage. The ideal man was married, strong and controlled.

Childbearing dominated the lives of women in the eighteenth century. It was childbearing in an unhygienic and medically primitive environment that killed large numbers of women. Cleanliness was not a high priority. Virtually no one bathed. What personal washing occurred was done from a basin. Most people simply scrubbed their faces with cold water. Most physicians were either self-trained or trained by another physician. No medical college existed in any of the colonies before the Revolution. Lack of knowledge of causes and cures of most diseases, effective medicines and painkillers and instruments such as the thermometer and stethoscope handicapped colonial doctors. The practice of bloodletting for almost any condition was universal. Doctors also employed emetics, diuretics and leeches. The cures often killed the patient.

John Carlyle, a wealthy merchant in Alexandria, had his life repeatedly scarred by the type of personal tragedy common to the eighteenth century. Of his eleven children, only two lived to adulthood. His first wife, Sarah, bore seven children, five of whom died in childhood. Sarah died in childbirth. Carlyle's second wife, Sybil, bore four children, only one of whom lived to be fifteen years old. This boy was killed while serving in the American Revolution. Bacterial stomach infections, intestinal worms, epidemic diseases, contaminated food and water and neglect and carelessness all contributed to a society in which 40 percent of children failed to reach adulthood.

By all accounts, George and Martha Washington enjoyed a happy marriage for some forty years. This was fortunate since options in cases of unhappy marriages were limited. A woman could win a separate maintenance if a husband's neglect or abuse made it clear that he was not fulfilling his husbandly duty to provide her adequately with clothing, food and shelter or if he was endangering her life. Once separated from her husband, a woman could try to make her own living, but her chances of achieving financial security on her own were not good. The situation for elite women was somewhat different. An elite wife who found her husband abusive or their marriage unhappy could usually finance an informal separation whereby she would live with friends and relatives.

There was rarely official religious or legal recognition that a marriage had collapsed. Any English subject could apply to the House of Lords in London for a divorce by means of a private Act of Parliament, but such a difficult and expensive procedure was out of the question for most people. The situation changed little after the Revolution. The first post-independence divorce in Virginia did not occur until 1803.

WHAT THEY WORE

In 1776, upper-class Virginians arrived at balls and celebrations in the most up-to-date fashions of the time. As early as 1724, Hugh Jones wrote in *The Present State of Virginia* that Williamsburg's leading families dressed like the gentry in London.

In the matter of hairstyles, colonial Americans took their cues from Europe. Marie Antoinette, queen of France, was the fashion icon of the day and set a fad for outlandishly tall, elaborately decorated wigs in the late 1700s. Her hairdressers created hairdos that often weighed five or more pounds and stood up to three feet high. Her wigs were imitated by other members of the French court and soon ladies of fashion throughout Europe and in the American colonies. The height of these styles was generally about one to one and a half times the length of the face, and they were styled in a pyramid shape. This high hairstyle, called the pouf, was created using "cushions" made of fabric or cork. The cushion was attached to the top of the head, and then natural and false hair was curled, waved or frizzed and piled over and around the cushion. The pouf was often styled into allegories of current events and was ornamented with ribbons, pearls, jewels, flowers and feathers, as well as ships, birdcages and other items that evoked the theme. Such elaborate hairstyles could be worn for days or weeks at a time and frequently became the home of insects. It was permissible to scratch the head with a special stick.

The hairstyles of most American women were generally not as extreme as those in Europe. With the coming of the Revolution, the passion for high hair began to wane in America. It seemed extravagant, wasteful and silly and raised suspicions of pro-British sympathies. Josiah Bartlett, a delegate to the Continental Congress, wrote to his wife in 1778 about "the Tory ladies…wearing the most enormous high head Dresses after the manner of the Mistresses and Whores of the British officers."

Women's gowns of eighteenth-century America usually had scooped necklines, sometimes with ruffles along the edges. Depending on what was available or affordable, gowns could be made of extravagant, expensive silk or simple cotton, wool and linen. The sleeves were most commonly three-quarter length, stopping at the elbow. A woman from a wealthy family in Virginia in the 1770s could have worn a silk gown from China, linen from Holland and footwear from England. Women wore stays (a bodice with strips of whalebone, metal or wood that gave the body proper definition) and hooped petticoats under their dresses. In the eighteenth century, women did not wear underwear. Stockings were made of cotton, silk or wool and held in place by garters tied above the knees. Shoes were made of silk, leather, linen and satin. Many women wore heels between one and two inches in height. Shoes were adorned with jewels, ribbons, bows, patterned fabric and beadwork. During Virginia's subtropical summers, many women chose washable linen or cotton clothing for informal wear. When the hot weather became unbearable, some women went without their stays for informal occasions and at home, although formal occasions still required them. Out of doors, a lady almost always wore a hat. A fashionable hat usually had a very shallow, flat crown and a wide brim. Fashionable women carried folding fans.

Tucked away in the recesses of Mount Vernon's archival vaults is a pair of avant-garde deep-purple silk high heels studded with silver sequins that Martha Washington wore on the day of her wedding to George Washington. Emily Shapiro, a former curator at Mount Vernon, described the shoes as a little sassy and definitely "over the top" for the time. "They were the Manolo Blahniks of her time."

At the time of her marriage to George Washington in 1759, Martha was twenty-seven and George was twenty-six. Martha was one of the wealthiest women in Virginia, having inherited five plantations when her first husband died. She was a bit of a clothes horse. Then, as now, if you had wealth, you flaunted it, making sure that you had the best clothes ordered from London in the deepest, richest colors. Such colors set the upper classes apart from poorer classes, who wore drab, homespun clothes in browns, beiges and tans.

We don't generally think of Martha Washington as a vivacious fashionista. She has come down to us after more than two hundred years as a frumpy, dumpy, plump, double-chinned Old Mother Hubbard type. There may be more design than accident in this portrayal of Martha Washington and the women of the Revolutionary War generation ("the Founding Mothers"). The new republic needed to make a clean break with the aristocratic ways of Europe and completely embrace simple republican virtues. Both George and Martha Washington were transformed by generations of historians into marble figures of rectitude whose dignity and decorum fostered a sense of legitimacy for the new country.

If one could not afford to import the latest fashions, it was possible to make clothes at home, and if this was not feasible, it was possible to buy American-made products. William Nelson of Yorktown wrote in 1770 that because of the American practice of boycotting British products as a form of protest, "They have already taught us to know that we can make many things for ourselves, and that we can do very well without many other things.…I now wear a good suit of cloth of my son's wool, manufactured as well as my shirts, in Albemarle [County], my shoes, hose, buckles, wig and hat, etc., of our own country, and in these we improve every year in quantity and quality."

The well-dressed urban gentleman in Virginia wore stockings or hose, breeches or trousers, a shirt, a waistcoat and jacket, a neck covering, ruffles at the wrists, a wig or powdered hair and a hat. A greatcoat or cloak was worn in bad weather. In rural areas of Virginia, men wore a mix of urban and frontier clothes. In 1776, Arthur Hopkins, of Pittsylvania County, owned among other things this curious mix of items: "1 Suit of black cloths, 1 Gray suit, 1 hunting shirt, 1 pair of buckskin breeches, 1 belt and tomahawk, 1 pair of silver shoe buckles, two silver watches made in London, and 1 pair of gold studs."

One foppish high-fashion style of dress that made its way from England to Virginia was the so-called Macaroni. One contemporary observer wrote, "They indeed make a ridiculous figure, with hats an inch in the brim, that do not cover, but lie upon the head, with about two pounds of fictitious hair, formed into what is called a club, hanging down their shoulders.…Their

A Macaroni was the embodiment of high fashion. Americans adopted the song "Yankee Doodle" as a song of defiance. *Courtesy of the Library of Congress.*

legs are at times covered with all colours of the rainbow; even flesh-coloured and green silk stockings are not excluded.…Such a figure, essenced and perfumed, with a bunch of lace sticking out under [the] chin, puzzles the common passenger." In 1774, Virginian James Mercer claimed that items had been stolen from him by a "profound knave" named William Foster Crosby, whom he described as "[dressed] like a Macaroni."

During the Revolution, British soldiers sang the ditty "Yankee Doodle," mocking Americans as simpletons who thought that if you stuck a feather in your cap you were the embodiment of high fashion. Americans adopted the tune as a song of defiance. By 1781, "Yankee Doodle" had become a song of national pride:

> *Yankee Doodle went to town*
> *A-riding on a pony*
> *Stuck a feather in his cap*
> *And called it macaroni.*
>
> *Yankee Doodle keep it up*
> *Yankee Doodle dandy,*
> *Mind the music and the step,*
> *And with the girls be handy.*

AMUSEMENTS

In 1770, despite the rising tide of political turmoil and the normal duties of making a living and raising a family, Virginians still found time (then as now) for fun. People of means were expected to be able to play an instrument or sing. Ladies did not generally play wind instruments, their garments being too restrictive. They could sing or play keyboards such as the forte-piano, the harpsichord or the spinet. Gentlemen often played the horn, flute or violin.

Dancing was an established social grace. Balls began with court dances like the minuet. These dances were performed in strict order of precedence, the ranking couple in the room dancing first and then down the social ladder. These were solo performances, watched carefully by the other guests. Pronounced stumbles and fumbles could cause a dancer to be banished for the social season. After the formalities, the floor was opened for general and less formal dancing.

A ball was a bit of a marathon. Guests might arrive at 7:00 p.m. for light refreshments and dancing. At 10:00 p.m., there might be a formal seated supper. Dancing resumed at midnight and might run to 5:00 a.m.

The dances of the common folk were not minuets but reels and jigs, accompanied not by string orchestras but by a single bagpipe or fiddle. Weddings, court days, log rolling, house raisings, corn shucking, harvestings and above all fairs provided occasions when any citizen could join in a host of amusements, including dancing. Physical sports such as footraces, wrestling, jumping contests, bowling and a version of modern soccer were played by the average citizens. Winners could receive prizes ranging from money to a bottle of liquor. Wealthier citizens ogled exotic animals, such as lions and camels, displayed at fairs. Everyone enjoyed performances of sleight of hand.

The first professional theater troupe arrived in Virginia from England in 1752 and opened with *The Merchant of Venice* in Williamsburg. William Verling started a troupe called the Virginia Company of Comedians in 1768 and performed many Shakespeare comedies among other works. Theaters were small and lit by candles. Historical plays like those of Shakespeare were enacted in contemporary dress, costuming being limited to turbans and other identifying accessories. Pastiche operas made their way into the playhouse and the houses of colonists looking for ways to entertain themselves at home. Philip Fithian's *Virginia Diary* records an informal evening concert in 1773 at Nomini Hall of *Artaxerxes*.

During winter months, people moved to their own homes or to public taverns for entertainment. A variety of games could be found in taverns, including whist, backgammon, chess, checkers, dice and dominoes. At home, women's quilting bees and sewing circles provided innocent and productive amusement, as did reading the Bible.

Letter writing was an important skill, for without it no communication was possible over a distance. Spelling was not yet standardized but rather phonetic, as evidenced by this letter written by Martha Washington:

Your letter of the 23d of November came to my hands yesterday—I am truly glad that the Major has had some little relief, and I trust ere this he has found ease from pain in his breast and side, I beg my dear Fanny to write one day in every week and then we shall know when to expect her letters—we are very anxious when the southern post comes to hear from you, I write to you by every Monday Post, your Letters comes to us on Satterday. I hope you will pay some attention to your own health as I feared you were in a very delicate situation when I left you at Mount Vernon—thank god we are all tolerable well hear tho I know you are with your friends that is ready to give you every assisstance and kindness—yet if there is any thing hear that you cannot get whare you are that you may want—I beg you will let us know and it will give us pleasure to supply you with it.

The diary of one of Virginia's most prominent citizens chronicled the most popular entertainments people indulged in prior to the Revolution. These included gambling (almost any activity could be turned into an occasion for gambling), dancing and cockfighting. In 1774, the Continental Congress clamped down on horse racing, gaming, cockfighting and other diversions apt to distract the people from the seriousness of the Patriot cause. Conformity to notions of republican virtue became the criteria on which to judge the suitability of amusements.

Despite the admonitions of the Continental Congress, balls continued to be held in the colonies throughout the American Revolution, with General Washington, an excellent dancer, being an eager participant. While visiting the general during the Revolution, Martha Washington attended the camp production of *Cato*, a tragedy by Joseph Addison. The play was performed by the staff officers for a "very numerous and splendid audience," including many officers and several of their wives. The play was received with enthusiasm.

PART IV

HOW THEY LIVED

Military Life

Militia and Minutemen

There was no standing army in colonial Virginia. Most people's lives were governed by the demands of farm chores and the seasons of planting and harvesting. Security alarms caused by pirates, raids by Native American tribes or incipient slave revolts were handled on an ad hoc basis. Riders would spread the alarm, and men would assemble to meet the challenge. The militia in Virginia was organized by county. In times of peace, the militia was more of a social or drinking club than a military organization. Discipline was lax and training sketchy. Even in times of war, militiamen were reluctant to serve more than a few weeks away from home. Without them, who would work the farm and provide for the family? Bounties were offered to attract the "idle poor," but these men often arrived without the required clothing, guns, powder and ammunition. The scarce equipment issued to these men was often "lost" or sold.

Notwithstanding the shortcomings of the militia, militiamen often provided essential manpower on the ground at key moments. British commanders had to take into account the size of militia forces operating against them when planning campaigns. Such forces might be unpredictable and unsteady in a pitched battle against British regulars, but they could inflict significant damage, especially in guerrilla-style attacks.

General Washington created the Continental army, which would serve the American war effort well, with the militia providing significant support. *Author's collection.*

Patriot militia units started forming in Virginia as early as 1774, notwithstanding the clear consensus at the First Continental Congress that economic sanctions were the preferred method of dealing with the British. On September 21, 1774, George Mason challenged this consensus by forming an independent company of volunteer militia. Mason persuaded a group of prominent citizens in Fairfax County that they must act. A resolution was adopted that declared:

> *In this Time of extreme Danger, with the Indian Enemy in our Country, and threatened with the Destruction of our Civil-rights, and Liberty, and all that is dear to British Subjects and Freemen; we the Subscribers, taking into our serious consideration the present alarming Situation of all the British Colonies upon this Continent as well as our own, being sensible of the Expediency of putting the Militia of this Colony upon a more respectable Footing, and hoping to excite others by our Example, have voluntarily freely & cordially entered into the following Association.... That we will form ourselves into a Company, not exceeding one hundred Men, by the Name of The Fairfax Independent Company of Volunteers.*

The company was to be made up of men of stature and financial means, and the officers were to stand for annual election. Mason explained that the company was meant to serve as a means by which future officers might learn the military arts. This was meant to provide the seed corn for future victories.

The urgency of the times is reflected in the observations of Nicholas Cresswell, a British visitor to Fairfax County, who wrote in October 1774:

> *Everything here is in the utmost confusion. Committees are appointed to inspect into the Characters and Conduct of every tradesman, to prevent them selling Tea or buying British Manufactures. Some of them have been tarred and feathered, others had their property burnt and destroyed by the populace. Independent Companies are raising in every County on the Continent… and train their Men as if they were on the Eve of War.…The King is openly cursed, and his authority set at defiance. In short, everything is ripe for rebellion. The New Englanders by their canting, whining, insinuating tricks have persuaded the rest of the Colonies that the Government is going to make absolute slaves of them.*

Prince William County also formed an independent militia company in the fall of 1774 and named it the Independent Company of Cadets. Loudon and Spotsylvania Counties formed their own independent militia companies in the early winter of 1774. By the end of 1774, six independent militia companies existed in Virginia, a small number considering the sixty-plus other counties and towns that still thought economic sanctions would be adequate to tame the British. The events of 1775 would further radicalize Virginia.

On July 17, 1775, the Culpeper Minutemen were organized, representing Orange, Fauquier and Culpeper Counties, and recruited some three hundred men. Originally, "Minuteman" referred to members of the New England militia who were known for being able to move out at a minute's notice. It was an old and well-established idea long before the Revolution. These minutemen were generally younger, had fewer family obligations and were provided with weapons by the local governments. In the early days of the war, it was thought that similar minuteman service would play an important part in Virginia's defense. A scheme was devised for this service to be the backbone of Virginia's defense, with eight thousand "citizen-soldiers" ready for service at short notice. The minute service in Virginia failed to attract popular recruitment or significant accomplishments with the exception of the heroic Culpeper Minutemen.

Considered frontiersmen at the time, the Culpeper Minutemen brought long rifles to the fight along with their reputations of being fearsome marksmen. In October 1775, the Minutemen were sent to Hampton to stop British ships from landing troops. The riflemen shot the sailors manning the ships and drove off the British flotilla. They next saw action in December at the Battle of Great Bridge, marching under their company flag, which featured a rattlesnake and the words "Liberty or Death" and "Don't Tread on Me." The victory at Great Bridge led to the expulsion of the royal governor. The Culpeper Minutemen disbanded in January 1776 under orders from the Virginia Committee of Safety, but many men continued on in the Virginia Line.

Even though the militia force was large and useful, General Washington was convinced that ultimate victory over the British would require the creation of a national, disciplined, professional army. He created this Continental army, which would serve the American war effort well, with the militia providing significant support.

THE VIRGINIA LINE

Regular United States infantry during the Revolutionary War were known as "Continentals" or the "Continental Line." The term "Virginia Line" refers to the quota of numbered infantry regiments assigned to Virginia at various times by the Continental Congress. Massachusetts and Virginia each furnished the largest of the state Lines. During the course of the war, Virginia was called on to raise fifteen regiments. The Virginia Line saw action in the northern campaigns and later in the Carolinas. The state was responsible for equipping its soldiers.

At the beginning of the war, equipping troops with proper firearms was a major problem. Although men usually brought their own weapons when mustered (long rifles or hunting guns), the lack of uniformity among these weapons was a problem. The notorious inaccuracy of the musket made the use of the bayonet a key element in battlefield tactics. The opposing armies lined up facing each other in ranks two or three deep and fired in the direction of the enemy. The musket was highly inaccurate at a distance greater than eighty yards. Speed in loading and firing was more important than aiming. The volume of fire was considered the measure of a good army. Presumably, if you fired enough times, you were bound to hit someone. The

Regular U.S. Infantry during the Revolutionary War were known as "Continentals" or the "Continental Line." *Courtesy of the Library of Congress.*

battlefield tactics of the time called for reliance on the musket with a bayonet. Civilian hunting guns and rifles were not designed to mount a bayonet. If a fight was confined to shooting, the Virginians had an advantage with their longer-range rifles. If a battle ended with a bayonet charge, of which the British were masters, the Virginians would be outmatched. In 1777, General Washington formed a Corps of Riflemen under the command of the Virginian Daniel Morgan to take advantage of the long-range shooting capability and accuracy of the rifle. These riflemen were a special unit, protected by regular Line troops when threatened by bayonets. The musket problem was not resolved until 1777. France became the primary supplier of military-style muskets. Some 102,000 muskets were delivered to America between 1776 and 1781. By 1777, the entire Virginia Line was equipped with French muskets.

After the final expulsion of Lord Dunmore, the royal governor of Virginia, the Virginia Line marched north to join General Washington's army around Boston. The British, driven from Boston, regrouped and attacked New York City in the late summer of 1776. Troops from Virginia made up one-third of

Washington's army, which fought a gallant but unsuccessful series of battles in defense of the city. The army then moved into New Jersey. Under pressure to revive flagging morale, General Washington came up with a daring plan to cross the Delaware River on Christmas night 1776 and attack the Hessian garrison at Trenton on December 26. The Virginians were among the first to cross the Delaware River. This small victory raised the morale of the Patriot forces.

By 1777, Washington's small army could only watch, wait and attempt to thwart any aggressive moves on the part of the British. In September, the British moved on Philadelphia, the seat of the Continental Congress. General Washington positioned his army along Brandywine Creek to block the British. On September 11, 1777, the British successfully outflanked the Patriot army and routed the Americans. Complete disaster was narrowly avoided when General Nathanael Greene established a rear guard with the American reserves. This force was predominantly made up of Virginians. The rear guard held the British off until sunset and then made an orderly withdrawal.

The British now had an open road to Philadelphia. Washington reorganized, followed the British and attacked at Germantown. Although the attack was initially successful, General Greene's command, including the Virginians, advanced too far and was cut off. The men fought their way out but suffered heavy losses. The British captured Philadelphia.

In order to monitor the British in Philadelphia, General Washington camped the army for the winter at Valley Forge. The enlistments for the Virginia regiments were about to expire, and the state was finding it difficult to recruit new men. Finally, Virginia was forced to send the First and Second State Line Regiments, which were originally intended only to be used within Virginia, to Washington at Valley Forge.

The British marched out of Philadelphia in the spring and summer of 1778, returning to New York City. The Americans attacked the British rear guard, but the Battle of Monmouth was indecisive. This was the last major battle of the Revolutionary War in the middle and northern states.

The Virginia Line was virtually obliterated in South Carolina in 1780. Almost all of the Virginians were captured when General Benjamin Lincoln surrendered his army of some five thousand men of the Continental army and militia at Charlestown, South Carolina, in May. More than 10 percent were Virginians.

Two Virginia units, coming as reinforcements, had not reached Charlestown before the surrender. Colonel Abraham Buford leading 380 men began to return to Virginia after learning of the surrender. They marched north too slowly and were overtaken by Banastre Tarleton's British Legion. Using sabers and bayonets, the British Loyalists won a crushing victory, killing and wounding 300 Americans at the cost of 20 Loyalists killed and wounded. Buford claimed that many of his men who had surrendered were massacred without mercy. Tarleton reported that when his horse was shot and he had been pinned on the ground, his men thought he had been killed and some of his troops acted with "vindictive asperity." The engagement became known in American circles as the "Waxhaws Massacre," and the phrase "Tarleton's quarter" was used to describe the practice of giving no quarter during battle and killing those who surrendered.

Virginia attempted to raise seven new regiments for the Line, but by August 1780, it could not field even one of these regiments. Virginia did supply Line regiments to the Southern Department by February 1781, and they took part in the Battle of Guilford Court House (North Carolina) on March 15, 1781.

FIFERS AND DRUMMERS

During the American Revolution, armies used music to communicate over long distances. In infantry units, the fife was used because of its high-pitched sound and the drum because of its low-pitched sound. Both instruments can be easily heard at great distances, even through the din of battle. Music gave instructions for advance or retreat and helped keep order on the battlefield. Drummers would play beatings telling soldiers to turn right or left, as well as to load and fire their muskets. There was a tune called "Cease Fire" that fifers and drummers played to instructs troops to stop firing. A tune called "Parley" was used to signal to the enemy that a surrender or peace talk was desired.

Fifers and drummers were used to help regulate camp life as well. Fife and drum calls signaled the commencement of daily tasks such as waking up, eating meals and performing camp chores.

Most musicians were either younger than sixteen or older than fifty. Once the uniform of the Continental army was regularized and in sufficient supply, musicians wore a distinct outfit. Musicians wore an opposite-colored coat than that worn by a combat soldier. If a combat soldier wore a blue coat with red cuffs, a musician would wear a red coat with blue cuffs. The

Armies used music to communicate over long distances, and officers depended on musicians to communicate orders to the troops. *Courtesy of the Library of Congress.*

distinctive uniforms of musicians made them easily identifiable on the battlefield, an important consideration since officers depended on musicians to communicate real-time orders to the troops.

Each company in an American infantry regiment during the Revolution (a full-strength company was made up of forty privates, three corporals, one ensign, one lieutenant and one captain) would have had one to two fifers and one to two drummers.

Fifer Thomas Cole served as a free African American in the First Virginia State Line for at least six years before he was discharged in 1783.

BLACK SOLDIERS IN THE REVOLUTION

During the American Revolution, the British lacked sufficient manpower to put down a revolt by a "people numerous and well-armed." This manpower shortage made the use of slaves all the more appealing to the British since slaves constituted some 20 percent of the total population of the colonies. On June 30, 1779, Sir Henry Clinton, the commander-in-chief of British forces in North America, promised in the so-called Philipsburg Proclamation that "every NEGRO who shall desert the Rebel Standard, [is granted] full security to follow within these Lines, any Occupation which he shall think proper." Now it was not hundreds of slaves seeking refuge in British lines, as they had done after Lord Dunmore's 1775 proclamation in Virginia, but rather tens of thousands. Some 100,000 enslaved people (out of an enslaved population of 500,000) are estimated to have sought freedom with the British over the course of the next four years. The number might have climbed even higher had slaves not feared brutal retaliation against their families if they fled from their enslavers.

By freeing the slaves, the British forced slave masters to guard slaves, one of their chief economic assets, instead of fighting British troops. The British were willing to emancipate slaves if by so doing they could first cripple and then crush the rebellion. Much as in the later American Civil War, military necessity rather than morality acted as the catalyst of history. The use of slaves by the British for military purposes soon prompted the American rebels to begin recruiting Black soldiers. George Washington gave his approval to Rhode Island's plan to raise an entire regiment of Black slaves (the state bought and emancipated slaves willing to become soldiers). Similarly, Massachusetts raised an all-Black unit, the Bucks of America, under Samuel Middleton, the only Black commissioned officer in the Continental army. In October 1780, even Maryland accepted "any able-bodied slave between 16 and 40 years of age, who voluntarily enters into service…with the consent and agreement of his master." New York began recruiting slaves in March 1781. By June 1781, some 1,500 (25 percent) of the 6,000 troops under George Washington's direct command were Black.

Hundreds of free and enslaved men from Virginia fought in the Patriot cause. Like the rest of the population, these men had their own motives for doing so. Some had no choice and were simply enlisted by their enslavers. Others could see a path to emancipation. Still others saw a possible avenue for economic advancement.

Take, for example, the case of Private Andrew Ferguson. Andrew Ferguson was born in Dinwiddie County in the early 1760s. Ferguson was born to free Black parents. Andrew and his father were captured by British forces who, assuming that they were enslaved, offered father and son freedom if they would fight for the king. They refused and were beaten for their obstinate refusal. The pair escaped from the British and joined the

Patriot forces. Andrew Ferguson was destined to see a great deal of action, in several theaters, during the war. He fought at Brandywine (Pennsylvania), at Kings Mountain (South Carolina) and at Cowpens (South Carolina). He was severely wounded at the Battle of Guilford Court House (North Carolina) but later fought at the Siege of Ninety Six and the Battle of Eutaw Springs (both in South Carolina). Andrew Ferguson served five years and six months.

Although Andrew Ferguson signed up voluntarily, William Lee had no such choice. George Washington bought William "Billy" Lee, his brother Frank and two other slaves in 1768. Billy Lee was eighteen. Frank became the butler at Mount Vernon, while Billy became Washington's valet. Billy also became the keeper of Washington's pack of hunting dogs.

Fox hunting was an important part of the social life of Virginia's gentry, and Billy Lee distinguished himself as a huntsman at Washington's side. An eyewitness described Lee during a hunt: "Will, the huntsman, better known in Revolutionary lore as Billy, rode a horse called *Chinkling*, a surprising leaper, and made very much like its rider, low, but sturdy, and of great bone and muscle. Will had but one order, which was to keep with the hounds; and, mounted on *Chinkling*…this fearless horseman would rush, at full speed, through brake or tangled wood, in a style at which modern huntsmen would stand aghast."

Washington took Billy Lee to war with him, where he served at Washington's side for eight years. After the war, between 1785 and 1789, Lee injured both of his knees and found himself back at Mount Vernon. William Lee was freed under the terms of Washington's will for "his faithful services during the Revolutionary War" and received a substantial pension for the remainder of his life and the option of remaining at Mount Vernon. Lee lived on at Mount Vernon until his death in 1811.

At least 140 Black men served in the Virginia Navy. Some of these were already experienced boatmen and pilots long before the war. An enslaved man named Cuffee was among this group of talented pilots. Cuffee learned how to navigate boats in Norfolk's bustling harbor. Cuffee was a pilot on the *Row Galley*, which was commanded by Captain James Barron, and was killed in the line of duty in 1781.

Another enslaved man, Mark Starlins, was a native African who had been trained as a pilot from his youth and showed particular bravery on the *Patriot* when he led the crew in an attack on a British sloop in the James River. He was engaged in daring night raids on British vessels in Hampton Roads during the spring and summer of 1781. After the war, Starlins was reclaimed by his master and died shortly thereafter, still in slavery.

Lewis Hinton enlisted on the *Dragon* for three years as a replacement for his owner, Thomas Hinton, who retired from the service due to failing health.

Pluto, the slave of Robert Brough of Norfolk, participated in many battles and in 1796 petitioned the General Assembly for his freedom, which he received.

Caesar Tarrant from Hampton was trained by his master as a ship's pilot, a trade many enslavers taught enslaved men in the Tidewater. Finding his services in demand at the beginning of the Revolution, Tarrant entered the Virginia Navy and served on the schooner *Patriot*. Tarrant participated in raids on British vessels in Hampton Roads, as well as south off the Virginia Capes. He was the pilot when his ship captured the British brig *Fanny* south of the Cape of Virginia. This was an uplifting victory for the Americans since the brig was loaded with supplies for British forces in Boston. Caesar Tarrant was able to gain his freedom and receive land after the war ended. Although money was important because it could be used to purchase land, it was land itself that was the ultimate symbol of wealth and freedom in the eighteenth century.

For the most part, enslaved men in the Virginia Navy had to be enlisted by their masters. Due to restrictions on slave recruits, there were many more free than enslaved Black men who served in the Virginia Navy. The desire for land bounties to be paid after the successful conclusion of the war may have motivated some of these men, just as it did many other recruits in the Revolutionary War. Joseph Ranger, a free Black, entered the Virginia Navy from Northumberland County in 1776. Joseph Ranger was to serve on the *Hero, Dragon, Jefferson* and *Patriot*. He served in the Virginia Navy throughout the war and even for six years beyond. In September 1783, Ranger received a land grant of one hundred acres from the Commonwealth of Virginia in the military district of Ohio. He was later to receive a military pension from the government of the United States.

There were several free Black Virginia families, including the Nickenses, Sorrels, Weavers, Woods, Stephenses and Haws who, as a result of supporting the Patriot cause, were able to obtain land that could be assembled into larger family estates. The Nickens family, from Lancaster County, had eight brothers and cousins fighting in the Patriot cause, both on land and sea: Amos, James, Edward, Hezekiah, John, Nathaniel, Richard and William. After the war, Richard, Edward, Hezekiah and Nathaniel Nickens received one hundred acres each. James, originally a sailor, switched to militia service and subsequently received two hundred acres. These lands were all located in the military district of Ohio.

Whether because of fear of the retribution of their enslavers or the hope of something better to come, 80 percent of America's enslaved population chose not to take up the British offer of immediate emancipation.

THE VIRGINIA NAVY

"In Virginia we have properly two frontiers," wrote Richard Henry Lee, "one bordered by a wilderness, the other by the Sea." The Chesapeake Bay borders Virginia for some two hundred miles. Additionally, four major rivers—the James, York, Rappahannock and Potomac—are navigable deep into the interior. This presented a definite security threat. The need for a navy was evident, especially when Lord Dunmore and his Loyalist forces began raiding towns and plantations along the rivers in the summer of 1775.

Late in 1775, Colonel Patrick Henry, on his own initiative, commissioned James Barron to arm a vessel and pursue two suspicious ships. In December, Virginia's Committee of Safety was authorized to arm as many vessels as necessary to protect Virginia's rivers. The Committee of Safety immediately purchased five vessels, including two small boats, a somewhat larger schooner and two large brigs. Virginia also bought vessels to serve as state-owned traders sent on voyages to the West Indies and Europe to procure gunpowder and other war materiel.

Throughout the war, vessels were bought and built. Particularly popular were row galleys, shallow-draft vessels that could maneuver using both oars and sails. These vessels were particularly well suited to coastal and river defense.

Manning the vessels proved difficult because the navy had to compete with privateers for manpower. The Virginia Navy officially commissioned seventy-seven vessels during the war, while one hundred Virginia vessels sailed as privateers, attacking enemy shipping for personal profit. The navy's view on prize distribution became more liberal as the war progressed and the manpower crisis grew worse. The percentage of a captured vessel's value going to the crew that took the prize rose from one-third for unarmed merchantman and one-half for an armed vessel to one-half for a merchantman and the entire value for a naval vessel. By October 1780, Virginia was promising crews the full value of any vessels they captured.

Nevertheless, the Virginia Navy always had more vessels than it could adequately crew. The navy could never compete with privateers, who from the first had the right to keep 100 percent of the value of the prize and could devote their full energies to taking prizes. The initially stingy navy was further hobbled by non-income-producing official tasks such as convoy duty, transporting troops and carrying messages, all tasks not likely to result in capturing rich prizes.

The navy recruited mainly in the Chesapeake Bay area and from counties bordering the major rivers. The median age of recruits was twenty-one in 1776 and twenty-six by the end of the war. About 2 percent of the naval force were enslaved men. Seaman William Bush was listed on the records as a "Public Negro," indicating that he was purchased by the state. Others were enlisted by their masters.

The Virginia Navy engaged in what might be termed maritime guerrilla warfare. Traditional naval battles in the eighteenth century involved two fleets lining up opposite each other and pounding each other with cannon fire, while trying to outmaneuver the enemy or break his cohesive line. The Virginia Navy never had ships large enough to engage in this type of warfare. The navy picked off lone merchantmen, attacked raiding parties or swarmed larger enemy privateer vessels, overwhelming them with numbers. If the British brought up major warships, the Virginia Navy retreated into shallow backwaters, where the larger warships could not follow.

The Virginia Navy was almost completely destroyed in a naval-land engagement on April 27, 1781, at the village of Osborne's, fifteen miles south of Richmond on the James River, by British and Loyalist troops under the command of Benedict Arnold. The British captured two ships, three brigs, two schooners and five sloops, all laden with tobacco, flour, cordage and other supplies. They burned or sank four ships, five brigs and several smaller vessels. Only three of the smallest vessels—the *Patriot*, the *Liberty* and the *Fly*—survived the debacle.

THE SOLDIERS OF THE KING

In 1775, the British army numbered forty-eight thousand men, about a quarter of the size of the French army. The island nation depended on the navy to maintain British trade and project British power. Throughout the war, the British could strike when and where they would along the virtually undefended American coastline. Unlike the navy, which depended on conscription and impressment for manpower, the British army at the time of the American Revolution was a volunteer force. Volunteers were farm laborers or the unemployed and usually in their early twenties. A life in the army provided steady pay, regular meals and an escape from poverty. The noncommissioned officers were the backbone of the army and ensured strict discipline and rigorous training.

As the war progressed, the army expanded rapidly. Some fifty thousand British soldiers fought in America. Two short periods of impressment were tried in which unemployed men were taken into the army. This proved so unpopular in Britain that it was quickly abandoned. The British turned to a well-established eighteenth-century custom to augment their numbers, namely hiring foreign auxiliaries. About thirty thousand German troops were hired by the British to fight during the American Revolution. Most of these troops were from the German princely state of Hesse-Cassel, hence the term "Hessians" came to be applied to all German troops in America no matter the princely state from which they originated.

Soldiers were a major export for Hesse-Cassel. Boys were registered for military service at the age of seven. Men from the ages of sixteen to thirty presented themselves annually for possible induction. School dropouts, bankrupts and the unemployed could be inducted at any time. Life in the Hessian army was marked by harsh discipline but had economic benefits. Wages were higher than farm work, and there was a promise of additional official money from the sale of captured military property. There was also the lure of making money by plundering civilians, which although officially forbidden was widespread.

Such widespread plundering made the Hessians unpopular with Americans and drove many neutral fence sitters to become ardent Patriots. The Declaration of Independence condemned the king for "transporting large Armies of foreign Mercenaries to complete the works of death, desolation and tyranny, already begun with circumstances of Cruelty and perfidy scarcely paralleled in the most barbarous ages, and totally unworthy the Head of a civilized nation."

Another source of manpower came from American Loyalists. Some twenty-five thousand Loyalists served the king during the war, most in homegrown regiments.

Virginia became a major repository for enemy prisoners of war. Because the British ruled the sea, prisoner of war camps were located far inland, where they would be immune from rescue attempts. The camps were located in rich farmland to facilitate the supply of food that the Americans were responsible for providing their prisoners.

At Charlottesville, the Convention army prisoners built wooden huts on what is today called Barracks Road. *Courtesy of the Library of Congress.*

Virginia's first prisoner of war camp was located at Dumfries and housed some fifty German auxiliaries captured at Trenton on December 26, 1776. These prisoners were subsequently marched to a more secure location in Winchester.

General John ("Gentleman Johnny") Burgoyne surrendered a British army at Saratoga, New York, in October 1777. The surrender terms documented in the "Convention of Saratoga" called for 5,900 British and German troops to march to Boston, where they would be shipped to England, with a pledge not to fight against the Americans again. The Continental Congress found a way to thwart the surrender terms and keep the prisoners. Congress insisted that the surrender articles be ratified by "the King and Parliament." This was an impossible condition since it implied British recognition of the legitimacy of the Congress and the independence of America.

In November 1778, the Convention army prisoners began a seven-hundred-mile march from Boston to Virginia. They were divided into six divisions, each marching one day behind the other. The prisoners crossed the Potomac River in late 1778 and passed through Leesburg, Prince William County, Warrenton, Culpeper County and Orange Court House before reaching Charlottesville, their final destination. At Charlottesville, the prisoners built wooden huts on what is today called Barracks Road.

While the common soldiers lived rough, the British and German officers were able to pay to rent private accommodations. British general William Phillips and the Hessian commander, Baron Friedrich von Riedesel, were treated more as guests than as prisoners. Thomas Jefferson played the violin with Baron Friedrich von Riedesel at Monticello. Baron Friedrich von Riedesel and General William Phillips were later exchanged for General Benjamin Lincoln.

In 1780, when the British began raiding into Virginia, Governor Thomas Jefferson had the British prisoners marched into Maryland. The 1,500 Hessian prisoners remained in the Charlottesville area. The American plan was to encourage the German auxiliaries to defect by having them work on farms with German-speaking settlers. Early in the war, the Continental Congress devised a plan offering fifty acres of land, freedom to practice their religion and civil liberties to German deserters. Thousands of former Hessian soldiers did indeed remain in America after the war.

The American-French victory at Yorktown in October 1781 saw a fresh infusion of prisoners of war. British and German prisoners were marched to Fairfax Court House, where they were divided into two groups. One group was sent to Maryland, while 3,029 prisoners (including 948 German auxiliaries) were marched to Winchester.

Despite his defeat at Yorktown, Lord Charles Cornwallis was cheered when he landed in England on January 21, 1782. He retained the confidence of successive British governments and was appointed governor-general and commander-in-chief in India in 1786. He successfully led British forces to victory in the Third Anglo-Mysore War from 1789 to 1792. In 1798, Cornwallis was appointed lord lieutenant and commander-in-chief of Ireland. The spirit of revolution had swept the British out of America and now threatened to do the same thing in Ireland. Disaffected Irishmen began to assert their "constitutional rights" and sought aid from the French, who had staged their own revolution in 1789. A massive force of twenty-six thousand was assembled under Lord Cornwallis, crushing the Irish rebellion and repulsing a French invasion of Ireland. Following his service in Ireland, Cornwallis was reappointed in 1805 to India, where he died of fever at the age of sixty-six not long after his arrival.

Another British soldier who returned to a triumphant welcome was Lieutenant Colonel Banastre Tarleton, who led the fearsome Loyalist British Legion. He was universally acclaimed for his legendary exploits in the American war and became a close friend of the Prince of Wales (the future King George IV). In 1787, Tarleton wrote *History of the Campaigns of 1780 and 1781 in the Southern Provinces of North America*. In 1790, he was elected to Parliament, where he served for more than twenty years. In the Napoleonic Wars, Tarleton served under the Duke of Wellington, reaching the rank of lieutenant general in 1801. In 1815, he was awarded a baronetcy.

In 2006, four Patriot regimental colors captured by Tarleton in 1779 and 1780 were auctioned by Sotheby's in New York City on Flag Day. Lot No. 1 consisted of one flag. Lot No. 2 consisted of the three regimental colors of the Third Virginia Detachment, which Tarleton captured at the Battle of Waxhaws (also known as the Waxhaws Massacre). Passed down in Tarleton's family for almost 250 years, these battle flags were the last American Revolutionary War colors known to remain in British hands and the last such colors to remain in private hands anywhere. The fiercely contested auction lasted fourteen minutes and raised $17.3 million. The three Virginia flags sold for $5 million. The private buyer remains anonymous, but the flags have occasionally been exhibited publically.

Unlike Cornwallis and Tarleton, Benedict Arnold was not celebrated when he arrived in England. He tried to advise British politicians to continue the fight for America despite the defeat at Yorktown. Members of Parliament expressed the hope that the government would never put Arnold at the head of a part of the British army, lest "the sentiments of true honour, which every British officer [holds] dearer than life, should be [offended]." Arnold next tried his hand at business. He was turned down for a position in the East India Company, where great fortunes were being made, with the explanation that the purity of his conduct was generally thought low. In 1785, Arnold tried land speculation in Canada and trading in the West Indies. The entire family moved in 1787 to Canada, where the quarrelsome Arnold became involved in a series of bad business deals and petty lawsuits. He became so unpopular that the townspeople of Saint John, New Brunswick, burned him in effigy in front of his house as his family watched. The family returned to London in 1791. In July 1792, Arnold fought a duel with the Earl of Lauderdale, who had impugned his honor. When war broke out with France, he outfitted a privateer and sailed for the West Indies. By 1801, Arnold's health had begun to fail. After four days of delirium, he died on June 14, 1801, at the age of sixty, leaving debts and a name synonymous with treachery.

PART V

PERSONAL STORIES
AND UNUSUAL EVENTS

EXTRAORDINARY WOMEN

CLEMENTINA RIND (1740–1774) was the first female newspaper printer and publisher in Virginia. Clementina's husband, William Rind, was a printer in Maryland and worked with a partner to produce the *Maryland Gazette*. The Rinds moved to Williamsburg in early 1766 after William Rind received an invitation to start the *Virginia Gazette*. The first issue of the *Gazette* appeared on May 16, 1766, under the motto, "Open to ALL PARTIES, but Influenced by NONE." The newspaper printed local advertisements as well as official information coming from the Virginia House of Burgesses. The press operated from a brick building that served as both a workspace and a home for Clementina, William and their five children.

William died in August 1773, leaving Clementina the sole support of the five children. Clementina Rind immediately took over management of the business without missing a single issue. She valued women as readers and began to print poetry, essays and vignettes of life in high society, along with the usual commercial and official news. The *Virginia Gazette* helped shape public consciousness on the eve of the American Revolution, as it became increasingly insistent on American rights.

Clementina Rind also printed the first edition of Thomas Jefferson's *A Summary View of the Rights of British America*, a work that brought Jefferson widespread attention as an early advocate of American independence.

In May 1774, the House of Burgesses appointed her public printer in spite of competition from rival male publishers. Unfortunately, in August, she fell ill and died at the age of thirty-four. Her obituary read, "a Lady of singular Merit, and universally esteemed."

HANNAH LEE CORBIN (1728–1782) is reputed to have been the first Virginia woman to take a stand for women's rights. She was born Hannah Lee, a member of the wealthy and influential Lee family of Stratford Hall in Westmoreland County. Two of her brothers, Francis Lightfoot Lee and Richard Henry Lee, were to become prominent American Patriots and signers of the Declaration of Independence.

Hannah married her cousin Gawain Corbin in 1747 at the age of nineteen. They had one daughter. Gawain Corbin died in 1760, leaving the thirty-two-year-old Hannah a rich widow, and so she would remain unless, as stipulated in her late husband's will, she remarried, in which case she would forfeit her inheritance. Being a woman of advanced thinking for the age, Hannah did not let this stipulation stand in her way. She began to cohabitate with her lover, a physician named Richard Hall. They had two children, to whom she gave the Corbin surname. Hannah's private life scandalized her family. She further aggravated her siblings by leaving the Anglican Church in 1764 and joining the Baptist Church.

The ever independent-thinking Hannah Corbin wrote to her brother Richard Henry Lee in 1778, echoing the very sentiments of "no taxation without representation" that animated the Revolution. "Why," she asked, "should widows pay taxes when they have no voice in making the laws or in choosing the men who made them?" She railed against male domination in law and politics and argued for women's suffrage. Like many whose lives did not reflect the promise of the Declaration that "all [people] are created equal," Hannah's Corbin's dream would have to wait. Women did not get the vote across America for almost 150 years after the Declaration of Independence.

ANNE MAKEMIE HOLDEN (1702–1788) was a wealthy widow in Accomack County. During the American Revolution, she supplied Patriot troops with corn and beef. As a woman, she was not permitted to vote, but she sought to preserve the ideals of the Revolution by deeding property to four of her male relatives with the proviso that they vote "for the most Wise and Discreet men who have Proved themselves real Friends to the American Independence" to represent Accomack County.

MARY WILLING BYRD (1740–1814) was the wife of William Byrd III of Westover in Charles City County. Hopelessly in debt, William Byrd committed suicide on January 1 or 2, 1777. As sole executrix, Mary Willing Byrd faced the enormous task of managing the estate and paying off her husband's huge debts. By selling off his western lands, as well as houses in Williamsburg and Richmond and a host of luxury items, she was able to safeguard her children's inheritance.

Taken up with immediate and pressing family business affairs, she tried to remain neutral during the American Revolution. This proved difficult. In the first week of January 1781, the British literally landed on her doorstep. A British force commanded by the detested traitor Benedict Arnold landed at Westover. Benedict Arnold's wife, Peggy Shippen, was Mary's cousin, which made some believe that Mary Byrd was a secret Loyalist. Notwithstanding the family connection, Mary Byrd and the family were confined to the upper stories of the house. The occupying army was not gentle with the property, trampling down the wheat, knocking down fences for firewood and butchering the farm animals.

Shortly after, the British decamped. A British naval lieutenant (a brother-in-law of Mary Byrd's sister), acting under a flag of truce, was detained by George Lee Turberville, an American major. The American major discovered a letter from Mary Byrd and a store of brandy, china and other goods destined for Westover. Byrd was charged with trading with the enemy. She defended herself eloquently against those who doubted her loyalty: "I wish well to all mankind, to America in particular. What am I but an American? All my friends and connections are in America; my whole property is here—could I wish ill to everything I have an interest in?" Her trial, scheduled to begin on March 15, was postponed until March 23 and ultimately dropped. Byrd had successfully protected both her reputation as a good American and her property.

ANNA MARIA LANE (1755–1810) joined the Continental army in 1776 with her husband, John. Lane's is the only documented case in Virginia of a woman dressing like a man and fighting on the battlefield during the Revolution. Lane and her husband fought side by side. The couple were on campaigns in New York, New Jersey, Pennsylvania and Georgia. Anna Maria received a severe wound at the Battle of Germantown (Pennsylvania) in 1777 that rendered her permanently lame. Despite her disability, she continued to fight alongside her husband and was with him when he was wounded during the Siege of Savannah in 1779. Husband and wife served until 1781. They then settled in Virginia.

In 1808, Virginia governor William H. Cabell asked the General Assembly to grant Anna Maria Lane a soldier's pension, writing that she was "very infirm, having been disabled by a severe wound which she received while fighting as a common soldier, in one of our Revolutionary battles, from which she never has recovered, and perhaps never will recover." The pension was granted, and the record notes that "in the Revolutionary War, [she] performed extraordinary military services at the Battle of Germantown, in the garb, and with the courage of a soldier."

Christiana Burdett Campbell (1723–1792) started her own business in Williamsburg in an age when this was very unusual for a woman. She was born Christiana Burdette, and her father was an innkeeper in Williamsburg, so it was natural for her to think of opening an inn in Williamsburg after the death of her husband, Ebenezer Campbell, in 1753. She rented several tavern locations before purchasing a permanent location in 1774. Christiana Campbell located her business close to the capitol building and catered to political figures such as George Washington, Thomas Jefferson and many members of the House of Burgesses.

Elizabeth "Betty" Zane (1765–1823) was a heroine of the Revolutionary War. In 1782, Native American and Loyalist forces attacked a small garrison of forty-two at Fort Henry in western Virginia (modern-day Wheeling, West Virginia). The garrison began to run out of black powder for the muskets and rifles. Zane immediately volunteered to leave the fort to retrieve a secret cache of powder. She ran fifty yards in full view of the enemy to retrieve the gunpowder. Her mad dash allowed American forces to hold the fort.

In 1861, John S. Adams wrote a poem titled "Elizabeth Zane" that immortalized Betty Zane and which reads, in part:

No time had she to waver or wait
Back must she go ere it be too late;
She snatched from the table its cloth in haste
And knotted it deftly around her waist,

Then filled it with powder—never, I ween,
Had powder so lovely a magazine;
Then scorning the bullets' deadly rain,
Like a startled fawn, fled Elizabeth Zane.

She gained the fort with her precious freight;
Strong hands fastened the oaken gate;
Brave men's eyes were suffused with tears
That had been strangers for many years.

THE STRANGE CASE OF HENRY WASHINGTON

Born on the Gambia River around 1740, Henry "Harry" Washington (real name unknown) was captured and sold into slavery sometime before 1763. He subsequently became the property of George Washington and was a groom in the stables at Mount Vernon. In November 1775, the royal governor of Virginia, Lord Dunmore, issued a proclamation offering freedom to any slave who would help put down the American rebels. That December, George Washington, commanding the Continental army in Massachusetts, received a report from his cousin Lund that Lord Dunmore's proclamation had stirred the passions of Washington's own slaves. "There is not a man of them but would leave us if they believed they could make their escape. Liberty is sweet." In 1776, Henry Washington escaped from Mount Vernon. He made his way to the British lines and joined Lord Dunmore's all-Black "Ethiopian Regiment." With several hundred men under arms, the Ethiopian Regiment fought for the Crown and the freedom of all Black people in slavery under the regimental motto, "Liberty to Slaves." Lord Dunmore's forces were overwhelmed in Virginia, and the Ethiopian Regiment disbanded. Henry Washington went on to serve in another Loyalist regiment, the Black Pioneers, under the command of Sir Henry Clinton as they moved from New York to Philadelphia to Charlestown, South Carolina, and, after the fall of Charlestown, back to New York.

Henry Washington was not alone in joining the British. The so-called Black Loyalists in the Revolutionary War are estimated to have numbered between 80,000 and 100,000 runaways who sought freedom within the lines of the British army. When the British evacuated Charlestown, hundreds of desperate former slaves tried to embark on the departing ships as slave catchers were sent in to return them to their enslavers. Some desperate people jumped from the docks and swam out to the last longboats ferrying passengers to the British fleet. Clinging to the sides of the longboats, they were not allowed on board, but neither would they let go; in the end, their fingers were chopped off.

In 1782, a provisional treaty granting the American colonies their independence was signed by Great Britain. As the British prepared for their final evacuation, the Americans demanded the return of runaway slaves under the terms of the peace treaty. The British refused to abandon Black Loyalists who had fought for the Crown to their fate. Some four thousand Black soldiers who had served the Crown during the war, together with their families, were listed in *The Book of Negroes*. Those lucky enough to make the list sailed to freedom in Canada and England. Among them was Henry Washington.

Henry Washington embarked on the ship *L'Abondance* in July 1783 with 405 other Black Loyalists, including women and children, bound for Nova Scotia. He was forty-three years old. His wife, Jenny, was twenty-four. Most of the Black Loyalists on board *L'Abondance* were followers of a blind preacher called "Daddy Moses" and settled as a community in a place they named Birchtown.

Life in Nova Scotia was hard. The Crown was slow in allocating land, the weather was harsh and the soil was rocky and poor. After several unhappy years in Nova Scotia, Henry Washington, together with his wife and three children and 1,192 other Black colonists, joined an enterprise sponsored by the Sierra Leone Company and financed by the British government that allowed Black Loyalist refugees to join the free Black community established in Sierra Leone in West Africa. In 1791, Henry Washington and his family settled in Sierra Leone. New settlers were promised twenty acres for every man, ten for every woman and five for every child. They were also given assurances that in Sierra Leone there would be no discrimination between white and Black settlers.

The company was long on promises and short on delivery. Relations between the company and the colonists deteriorated to the point that the company sought a royal charter from the British Parliament that would give the company formal jurisdiction over Sierra Leone. The company wanted full judicial authority to suppress dissent. The company explained, "[T]he unwarranted pretensions of the disaffected settlers, their narrow misguided views; their excessive jealousy of Europeans; the crude notions they had formed of their own rights; and the impetuosity of their tempers" would soon produce a "ruinous effect."

The settlers, who regarded themselves as loyal British subjects, petitioned the king, explaining how the Black settlers had been given land by the British government as a consequence of "our good behavior in the last war." The king, hearing of their unhappiness about living in a cold country, offered to "remove us to Sierra Leone where we may be comfortable." Things had not turned out in accordance with the terms of His Majesty's offer, and the settlers sought redress. The company ensured that the settlers' petition never reached the king.

By 1799, Sierra Leone's settlers had grown so discontented, so revolutionary in their rejection of the company's rule over the colony, that some in London likened them to the revolutionaries in France. The company noted with alarm "meetings of a most seditious and dangerous nature." The governor sent armed marshals to arrest several men on charges of treason. Within a week, thirty-one men were in custody. A military tribunal was set up to try the prisoners for "open and unprovoked rebellion." Henry Washington and twenty-three others were banished to the colony's desolate northern shore.

The exiles elected Henry Washington their leader in 1800, only months after George Washington's death at Mount Vernon. In the love of liberty, Henry Washington was not excelled by the better-known George Washington.

The Marquis and the Spy

An enslaved man in New Kent County known as James Armistead, upon learning that slaves who served the American cause could apply for freedom when the war ended, asked his owner, William Armistead, an ardent Patriot, if he could volunteer to serve with the Marquis de Lafayette's army defending Virginia against the British invasion of 1781. William Armistead agreed.

Lafayette, a longtime opponent of slavery who once wrote to George Washington, "I would never have drawn my sword in the cause of America if I could have conceived that thereby I was founding a land of slavery," found James Armistead very able and offered him a dangerous mission, namely to spy on the British. Posing as a runaway slave, Armistead made his way to the camp of the traitor Benedict Arnold at Portsmouth. Armistead offered his services as a guide and forager. The British accepted him.

James Armistead must have been a very persuasive individual because not only did he earn the trust of Benedict Arnold, but he also soon gained the trust of General Lord Cornwallis. Cornwallis made Armistead an orderly, which put him in the rooms where British military plans were being discussed. Armistead passed that information to fellow spies, who sneaked through the lines to deliver the intelligence to Lafayette.

In a strange turn of events, Lord Cornwallis soon asked Armistead to spy on the Americans. He took up the offer and was now in the position of

The Marquis de Lafayette found James Armistead able and offered him a dangerous mission, namely to become a spy. *Courtesy of the Library of Congress.*

being able to supply the Americans with accurate information about British plans and capabilities, while feeding the British misinformation. Armistead's reports to Generals Lafayette and Washington were vital to the American victory at Yorktown.

After Yorktown, Armistead returned to the plantation on which he was enslaved. Although Virginia passed a manumission act in 1782 allowing any slave who fought in the Revolution to apply to become free, subsequent legislation limited manumission to slaves who had carried guns and been soldiers. Since James served as a spy rather than a soldier, he was not eligible for emancipation. His first petition was ignored.

James Armistead tried again in 1786. This time, his petition was strongly supported by his owner, William Armistead, now a member of the House of Delegates, and by a personal testimonial from the Marquis de Lafayette in favor of granting freedom based on service during the war. On January 9, 1787, James was declared a free man. Upon receiving the news, he added "Lafayette" as his surname and was thereafter known as James Armistead Lafayette. James Armistead Lafayette became a successful farmer near Richmond and at one time owned several slaves. He was later granted an annual pension for his service during the Revolutionary War.

In 1824, the now sixty-seven-year-old Marquis de Lafayette returned to the United States at the invitation of President James Monroe. His year-long tour of all twenty-four states was a magnificent patriotic celebration. He was escorted between cities by the state militia and would enter each town through newly built triumphal arches to be welcomed by huge crowds. There were special events, patriotic speeches and celebratory dinners.

One of the cities Lafayette visited was Richmond. While making his way through the throngs of people in Richmond, he suddenly ordered his carriage to stop. Lafayette had seen his old comrade in arms James Armistead in the crowd. The Marquis de Lafayette left his carriage and made his way on foot through the crowd. After a separation of more than forty years, the two old veterans embraced.

Loyalists and the Unusual Fate of the Fairfax Family

Most of the citizens of Virginia found themselves on the winning side at the end of the Revolution, but an unlucky few did not.

Particularly unlucky were those Loyalists who actively took up arms or plotted against the Patriot cause. They suffered all of the pent-up rage that accompanies civil war. The houses of such Loyalists were burned and their property seized. A particularly glaring example occurred in southwest

Virginia in 1780. A Patriot spy uncovered a Loyalist plot to sabotage Virginia's all important lead and saltpeter mines in the area and then march on Charlottesville to free British prisoners of war. Governor Thomas Jefferson ordered Judge Charles Lynch to arrest the ringleaders and send the guilty to Richmond for trial. Lynch arrested seventy-five suspected Loyalists and brought them to his plantation, called Green Level, some twenty-five miles south of present-day Lynchburg. Judge Lynch decided to administer his own version of summary frontier justice. A few of the accused were acquitted, but many others were imprisoned for terms ranging from one to five years. The ringleaders were tied by their thumbs to the branches of a black walnut tree and given thirty-nine lashes with a cat o' nine tails whip. If the convicted Loyalist begged for mercy with the cry "Liberty forever," he was cut down and forcibly impressed into American military service. In 1782, the Virginia General Assembly immunized Lynch from legal action that might have arisen because of his extralegal methods of dealing with Loyalists. The General Assembly found that the measures taken by Judge Lynch were warranted given the emergency situation.

Other Loyalists suffered confiscation or exile. Robert Bristow of Prince William County, for example, remained loyal to the Crown and had 7,500 acres confiscated. The tract was divided into 100-acre lots and sold at auction. The present town of Brentsville stands on this land.

Jonathan Boucher came to the Chesapeake region as a young man. Starting out as a tutor for wealthy families, he eventually became an ordained minister. He became a close friend of George Washington and the tutor of Washington's stepson John Parke "Jacky" Custis. Notwithstanding his friendship with Washington, Boucher was an ardent Loyalist. He saw the trouble in America as arising from the personal resentments of a small group of malcontents who usurped extralegal powers and were misleading and intimidating an ignorant public. Boucher was so outspoken in the face of hostile crowds that he was forced to have pistols ready at hand in the pulpit. He returned to England unrepentant and later dedicated *A View of the Causes and Consequences of the American Revolution* (1797) to George Washington. This work consisted of thirteen sermons he had preached in America urging loyalty to the Crown. Washington sent a polite acknowledgement.

John Camm, another Anglican priest, was by 1772 president of the College of William and Mary, rector of Bruton Parish Church in Williamsburg and a member of the Royal Council of Virginia. Because of his steadfast loyalty to the king, he lost all three positions in the upheaval.

Most Virginians found themselves on the winning side at the end of the Revolution, but Loyalists suffered. *Courtesy of the Library of Congress.*

John Randolph served as king's attorney for Virginia. He was part of the influential Randolph family. His father, Sir John Randolph, was the only colonial Virginian ever to be knighted. During the Revolution, John Randolph remained loyal to the king, unlike his brother, Peyton Randolph, and his son, Edmund Randolph. John Randolph boycotted the Virginia Convention, headed by his brother, considering it an illegitimate and illegal assembly. When fighting broke out, John Randolph fled to England.

Merchant Archibald McCall was what you might call a pragmatist. He initially supported the king, insisting that his customers pay the British tax levied by the Stamp Act of 1765. He was tarred and feathered by a Patriot mob for his trouble. By 1770, he had learned his lesson and signed the Virginia Nonimportation Resolutions along with such prominent Patriots as George Washington. As the crisis got ever closer to war, McCall may have been selling food to the forces of the royal governor—he was certainly accused of having done so. Although he was exonerated by the Essex County Committee of Public Safety, there were still suspicions that McCall was a secret Loyalist. McCall sailed for England in 1775 for what was to be a short visit to his daughter. Believing that the war would be brief, McCall perhaps thought he would return after a short interlude and then get on the right side of the winning party. His plan went awry when the British Parliament enacted a law restricting travel from Britain to the American colonies. McCall finally returned to Virginia in 1783, avowing his ever-steadfast loyalty to the new country and setting about reclaiming his estates, which he successfully achieved. His 1814 obituary noted, "Mr. McCall was distinguished for the sagacity of his mind, and the cheerfulness of his manners."

One of the biggest losers was the Fairfax family. Thomas Fairfax was made Lord Fairfax of Cameron in the Peerage of Scotland on May 4, 1627. Another Thomas, the 6th Lord Fairfax, succeeded to the title in 1709, at which time he came into the family estates in Virginia, some 5 million acres. The 6th Lord Fairfax moved to Virginia to oversee the source of his wealth. Lord Fairfax was the only British peer to take up permanent residence in North America.

In 1748, Lord Fairfax employed the sixteen-year-old George Washington, a distant relative, to survey his lands in western Virginia. During the American Revolution, Lord Fairfax remained loyal to the Crown but did not leave America. His lands were confiscated, and the eighty-eight-year-old peer died less than two months after Washington's victory at Yorktown in 1781.

George William Fairfax was second cousin to Lord Fairfax. He became a mentor to George Washington, eight years his junior. Washington became a frequent visitor to Belvoir, the estate of George William Fairfax and his wife, Sally Cary Fairfax. Washington was said to have been quite smitten with Sally Fairfax before his marriage to Martha Dandridge Custis in

1759. The couples became great friends and remained close until George William and Sally returned to England in 1773 to attend to family business matters. George William entrusted his friend Washington to rent the Belvoir estate and sell some of his property. In 1774, Washington wrote to George William Fairfax about business matters. He also described the growing political tensions and assured his friend that he would keep the secret that George William was not returning any time soon. In fact, George William, a Loyalist, did intend to return but only when the political troubles were settled. The war settled the relationship of colony and mother country, and George William Fairfax was financially ruined as a result.

George William's brother Bryan had a strange destiny. Bryan was a fence sitter, as were almost one-third of the population of the colonies. Initially, he mildly debated the pros and cons of the political situation with George Washington and others, but by 1777, he was ready to pull up stakes and return to England, at least long enough to be ordained as an Episcopal priest.

Bryan Fairfax wrote to Washington:

> *For the past two years I have had a strong Desire to enter into Holy Orders than ever I had before tho' frequently in my Life have had the same, yet generally suffered worldly considerations to interfere. This Desire and the not finding myself at Liberty to concur in the Public measures make me very anxious to get to England, and I have been in Hopes of obtaining a Pass from the Congress…for that Purpose. There has appeared to me but one Objection, and that is, the giving of Intelligence, but I would not only enter into Engagements in that respect if required but it may* [be] *considered that what I might say would be of little Consequence, but if of any would rather of America because I really think that it would be the Interest of Great Britain to let her enjoy her Independence.*

Washington responded, "The difference in our political Sentiments never made any change in my friendship for you, and the favorable Sentiments I ever entertained of your honour, leaves me without a doubt that you would say any thing, or do any thing injurious to the cause we are engaged in after having pledged your word to the contrary."

Upon the death of 6th Lord Fairfax in Virginia in 1781, the title descended to his only surviving brother, Robert, who received cash compensation from the British Parliament for the loss of property during the Revolution. The settlement was a small fraction of the value of the family's confiscated land. Robert died in 1793, at which point Bryan Fairfax, having returned to

Virginia, claimed and was granted the title 8th Lord Fairfax by the British House of Lords. Bryan Fairfax became the first American-born holder of a British peerage, although he did not actually use the title, choosing the life of an Episcopal priest in Alexandria.

In 1802, Thomas Fairfax inherited the title 9th Lord Fairfax of Cameron after his father's death. He lived the life of a country squire, overseeing his forty thousand acres. His grandson Charles succeeded to the title. Charles's brother, John, succeeded his childless brother, becoming the 11th Lord Fairfax of Cameron.

By the late nineteenth century, the family had largely forgotten about the title. This all soon changed. In 1900, Albert Kirby Fairfax succeeded his father. In 1901, he was summoned to attend the funeral of Victoria, the queen empress of the British empire, ruler of one-quarter of the world's territory and people. The Committee of Privileges of the House of Lords confirmed Albert Fairfax as the rightful 12th Lord Fairfax of Cameron. The newly recognized Lord Fairfax became a naturalized British subject on November 17, 1908. The family resettled in Britain after an interlude of some 150 years.

Nicholas John Albert Fairfax is now the 14th Lord Fairfax of Cameron.

THE PAUL REVERE OF VIRGINIA

Virginia experienced a spate of military activity early in the Revolutionary War. Lord Dunmore, the royal governor, fought to keep the colony loyal to the Crown. Overconfident after an easy victory at Kemp's Landing, Lord Dunmore ordered an attack on Patriot forces near Norfolk. Only after a fierce battle ending in the destruction of Norfolk was Dunmore expelled. Lord Dunmore's army evacuated Norfolk, embarking on British ships. Smallpox broke out on the crowded ships even as the fleet left Virginia waters bound for New York.

Three years of relative peace followed. Virginia's false sense of security was rudely shattered in 1779 by a British expedition under Admiral Sir George Collier that raided and occupied the port cities of the Tidewater. In 1781, the British stepped up operations in the Southern theater of war. Benedict Arnold and a British fleet ravaged the Tidewater of Virginia, burning cities, seizing crops and destroying everything that they could find. Later in the year, Lord Cornwallis swept northward into Virginia and began to lay the country to waste. His only opposition was a small American force under the Frenchman Lafayette. The Virginia General Assembly abandoned Williamsburg, Richmond and Petersburg, fleeing to Charlottesville. The Virginia delegates decided to assemble in mid-June. The British hatched a plan to capture or kill the entire Virginia Assembly and Governor Thomas Jefferson in one lightning raid that would crush all opposition. Lord Cornwallis chose the savage Banastre Tarleton and his battle-hardened cavalry to do the job.

On the night of June 3, 1781, twenty-seven-year-old John "Jack" Jouett spotted Tarleton's cavalry near Cuckoo Tavern in Louisa County. Suspecting that the British were marching on Charlottesville, Jouett mounted his horse at 10:00 p.m. and began the forty-mile ride to Charlottesville. Traveling only with the light of the moon, Jouett took rough backwoods trails, riding hard to outdistance the British.

At 11:30 p.m., Tarleton paused for a three-hour rest at Louisa Courthouse. The British resumed their march at about 2:00 a.m. and soon encountered a train of thirteen Patriot supply wagons at Boswell's Tavern bound for South Carolina. Tarleton burned the wagons and continued toward Charlottesville.

At 4:30 a.m., Jack Jouett ascended the mountain on which Monticello sits. An early riser, Thomas Jefferson was in the gardens at Monticello when Jouett arrived. Jefferson fortified Jouett with a glass of Madeira wine and sent him on the two additional miles to warn the town of Charlottesville.

Jefferson did not rush to make an escape. He had breakfast and spent two hours gathering up important papers, all the while checking the path up the mountain with his telescope for signs of the British. When Jefferson finally spotted the British, he mounted a horse and headed into the woods, successfully eluding capture.

Thanks to Jouett's timely warning, most of the Virginia legislators in Charlottesville also escaped capture. Tarleton only managed to capture seven assemblymen, whom he later released as being of no importance. One of these Virginia representatives was Daniel Boone.

The Personal Woes of George Washington

Mason Locke Weems (1759–1825), known to history as Parson Weems, wrote *The Life of Washington* in 1800. Weems wrote the biography to amplify his subject. His subject was "Washington, the hero, and the demigod." It has been said of his writing, "If the tales aren't true, they should be. They are too pretty to be classified with the myths." Sometimes it is hard to think of George Washington as a man because of what Parson Weems and other earlier biographers wrote. But even while he was at the epicenter of political and military life, Washington was afflicted with personal problems.

Take, for example, his teeth. Despite his best efforts to care for his teeth, Washington lost his first tooth at the age of twenty-four. Almost every year thereafter, Washington suffered from severe toothaches, followed by the painful extraction of the teeth. Washington's teeth continued to deteriorate, making it hard for him to chew without pain. In 1773, at the age of forty-one, Washington wrote to a London merchant thanking him for his gift of two large stone jars of pickled tripe, which is soft and easy to eat. By the age of forty-nine, the year of the Battle of Yorktown, Washington was wearing false teeth wired to his remaining ones. By the time he was fifty-seven and sworn in for the first time as president of the United States, Washington had one remaining real tooth.

Far worse than an annoying physical ailment was the death of a beloved child. George Washington married Martha Dandridge Custis on January 6, 1759. He was twenty-six to her twenty-seven. Washington suddenly found himself responsible for a ready-made family: Martha Parke "Patsy" Custis, aged two, and John Parke "Jacky" Custis, aged four. In addition to the normal duties of a father in terms of providing love, warmth and sympathy, George Washington was also charged with being the administrator of the children's business affairs, which were not inconsiderable, considering that their late father, Daniel Parke Custis, was perhaps the wealthiest man in Virginia. Martha Washington herself was required to relinquish her rights in the dower share of her late husband's estate to the management of her new husband. If unmarried, Martha would have received one-third of Daniel Parke Custis's estate for her use and maintenance during her lifetime. As it was, the use of this money was left to the decisions of her new husband, George Washington. By all accounts, George Washington was not only a loving husband and stepfather but also a conscientious guardian of the property rights of both his wife and her children.

The stage was set for familial peace and tranquility, but fate took a hand. By the time Patsy was eleven, she was plagued with seizures. Patsy was afflicted with epilepsy. The progression of Patsy's epilepsy can be traced in George Washington's diaries, but only with difficulty. Washington's diary entries are sparse and never betray his inner emotions, which were under tight control.

George and Martha Washington were willing to try almost anything, even improbable folk remedies. The distraught parents relied, mainly, on conventional eighteenth-century medical treatments for epilepsy. This was doomed from the start. The doctor's principal role at that time was to provide comfort and support, set broken bones and prescribe herbal remedies. Theories of medicine at the time were based on the notion that disease was caused by an imbalance in bodily "humors," or fluids. The Washington family consulted numerous doctors to no avail. Patsy's seizures increased. George Washington kept a log of these episodes. During an eighty-six-day period, Patsy had seizures on twenty-six days.

Around four o'clock in the afternoon on June 19, 1773 (some six months before the Boston Tea Party), after everyone had finished dinner, Patsy (then aged seventeen) and a girl friend were talking quietly. Patsy went to her room to retrieve a letter. Hearing a strange noise coming from Patsy's room, her friend found Patsy in the throes of a life-threatening seizure.

Martha Washington was frantic. George Washington knelt beside his beloved stepdaughter, whom he had raised from infancy, with tears running down his cheeks. She was dead within two minutes.

In a letter to his brother-in-law written the following day, George Washington relayed the news that Patsy, described as his "Sweet Innocent Girl," had been buried earlier in the day and that the situation had "reduced my poor Wife to the lowest ebb of Misery."

George Washington also had to deal with a "problem child." Washington's stepson, John Parke "Jacky" Custis, was destined to inherit his late father's huge fortune. George Washington wanted to make sure that the boy was prepared for the responsibilities that so much wealth entailed.

Jacky's early education was initially handled by his mother, Martha. But in 1761, when the boy was about seven, a Scottish tutor named Walter Magowan was brought to live at Mount Vernon to begin Jacky's formal education. Unfortunately, the boy was lazy and headstrong and had no interest in his studies.

In 1768, Jacky was sent away to a boarding school in order to prepare him for college. George Washington wrote to Reverend Jonathan Boucher, an Anglican minister who ran the school for boys, noting that Jacky had been introduced to both Greek and Latin by his tutor and described his stepson as a boy "about 14 yrs. of age, untainted in his morals, and of innocent manners." He considered him "a promising boy" and expressed "anxiety" that as "the last of his Family," who would be coming into "a very large Fortune," he wanted to see the boy made "fit for more useful purposes, than a horse Racer."

The next five years were frustrating for both George Washington and Reverend Boucher. When Jacky Custis was sixteen, Washington wrote to Boucher that his stepson's mind was wholly centered on "Dogs, Horses, and Guns," as well as "Dress and equipage." Boucher was unable to give Washington any reassurances, noting that young Jack "does not much like books." Warming to his subject, Boucher reported that Jack was the laziest boy he had ever known and also "so surprisingly voluptuous: one would suppose Nature had intended Him for some Asiatic Prince."

Jacky was always full of surprises. In 1773, he announced his engagement to fifteen-year-old Eleanor Calvert, who came from a prominent Maryland family. Washington was outraged; Martha was delighted. Washington was initially able to convince the young couple to postpone the marriage until after Jack had finished college and could "thereby render himself more deserving of the Lady and useful to Society." Jack lasted a few months at King's College (now Columbia University) in New York City before bolting for home. On February 3, 1774, Jack, now nineteen years old and Eleanor, sixteen, were wed.

Prospects for the young couple were bright. After all, Jack had inherited an enormous fortune. But what the father had made, the son could not keep. Jack bought a plantation called Abingdon in Fairfax County, Virginia. The seller, Robert Alexander, took every advantage of the inexperienced and impetuous Jack. When he learned of the terms of the purchase, George Washington informed Custis that "[n]o Virginia Estate (except a few under the best management) can stand simple Interest how then can they bear compound Interest?"

George Washington wrote in 1778, "I am afraid Jack Custis, in spite of all of the admonition and advice I gave him about selling faster than he bought, is making a ruinous hand of his Estate." By 1781, the financial strains of the Abingdon purchase had almost bankrupted Jack Custis.

No hand at business, Jack Custis proved himself equally poor at politics. In 1778, he was elected to the Virginia House of Burgesses as a delegate from Fairfax County. Taking time out from his duties as a general in the field, commanding the Continental army and engaged in a desperate war, Washington wrote to the young politician, "I do not suppose that so young a senator as you are, so little versed in political disquisition, can yet have much influence in a popular assembly, composed of various talents and different views, but it is in your power to be punctual in attendance." Custis won reelection but missed assignments to important committees because of his habitual late arrival, usually the result of personal matters.

Despite Washington's frequent criticism of Jack, the young man described their relationship fondly. Custis wrote to Washington, "It pleased the Almighty to deprive me at a very early Period of Life of my Father, but I cannot sufficiently adore His Goodness in sending Me so good a Guardian as you Sir." He went on to assure Washington, "He best deserves the Name of Father who acts the Part of one."

As the Revolutionary War came to a close, Custis persuaded Washington to allow him to join the general's suite at Yorktown as a "civilian aide-de-camp." This turned out to be another unfortunate choice. Soon after the British surrender, Jack was stricken with the contagious fever spreading throughout the crowded army camps. On November 5, 1781, shortly before his twenty-seventh birthday, John Parke Custis died.

The Plot to Kidnap Benedict Arnold

Sergeant Major John Champe (1752–1798) was a senior enlisted soldier in the Continental army serving in the Virginia cavalry under "Light-Horse Harry" Lee. In October 1780, "Lee's Legion" was encamped near Bergen, New Jersey, a few miles from the Hudson River. It was here that Champe, a native of Loudon County, became involved in one of the most fantastic plots of the war—namely, the kidnapping of the traitor Benedict Arnold.

In September 1780, Arnold's plot to surrender the stronghold of West Point (and possibly George Washington as his prisoner) to the British unraveled. Arnold fled to the British and was rewarded with cash and the rank of brigadier general in the British army. George Washington wanted the traitor brought before him alive—"My aim is to make a public example of him." Washington's plan called for a soldier to cross the Hudson River and present himself in New York as a deserter. With the aid of spies already in New York, this secret agent would then kidnap Arnold and bring him back across the Hudson into American lines. Did General Lee know of a man up to the task? Indeed he did, one John Champe, who "was about twenty-three or twenty-four years of age, had enlisted in 1776, rather above the common size, full of bone and muscle, with a saturnine countenance, grave, thoughtful, and taciturn, of tried courage and inflexible perseverance."

Champe was intrigued with the plan, which he found "powerful and delicious." Champe was not concerned with the danger but was troubled by the idea of being seen as a deserter. General Lee assured Champe that his reputation would be protected if the enterprise failed. And so the die was cast. On the night of October 20, 1780, John Champe rode off with his arms to desert to the British. An American patrol spotted him, and when he did not halt when given the command, the patrol gave chase. Only moments ahead of the pursuing patrol, Champe plunged into the Hudson River and swam toward a British warship. The warship sent a boat to pick him up and fired on the pursuing Americans.

Champe was questioned by a series of ever-higher-ranking British officers, to whom he told the same story over and over. Men like himself were following Benedict Arnold's example. The morale among American troops was low. The British already believed that disaffection was rampant in Washington's army and so were only too willing to believe Champe's story.

He was introduced to Benedict Arnold, who made Champe one of his recruiting sergeants for the Loyalist "American Legion." Champe now had continuous access to Arnold's house overlooking the Hudson River. Champe sent General Lee his plan to abduct the traitor. Arnold's fenced garden overlooked the river, and Arnold strolled in the garden every night before he went to bed. Champe intended to pry fence boards loose and, with the help of one of Washington's spies already in the city, tie and gag Arnold and drag him to a waiting small boat. If stopped by anyone, Champe would say that they were taking a drunken soldier to the guardhouse.

The plan soon went awry. The day before the planned abduction, Arnold moved his quarters to another part of Manhattan, taking Champe, his recruiter, with him. Soon after, Arnold's American Legion sailed to join other British units in an invasion of Virginia. After sailing up the James River, Arnold and his invasion force took Richmond. The British moved freely about Virginia, burning and pillaging. Washington's attitude toward Arnold hardened, and he no longer worried about Arnold becoming a martyr. After ordering Major General the Marquis de Lafayette to Virginia to confront the invaders, Washington ordered that if Arnold were captured, he was to be summarily executed.

Back in his native Virginia, John Champe found himself in the odd position of fighting with Arnold's troops, sometimes against his old commander, General Lee. Finally, Champe was able to escape through British lines and make his way to the Appalachian Mountains, eventually returning to "Light-Horse Harry" Lee's command. When Lee's men learned the true story, they showed Champe "love and respect" for his "daring" adventure, Lee wrote years later in his memoir.

Stories of Life and Valor

William Campbell (1745–1781) was one of the thirteen signatories of the Fincastle Resolutions, one of the statements of resistance to the acts of the British Crown after the Boston Tea Party. An ardent Patriot and husband of Patrick Henry's sister, Elizabeth, Campbell was promoted to colonel of militia in 1780 and led his men at the Battle of Kings Mountain (South Carolina) with the battle cry, "Shout like hell and fight like devils." He was known for his harsh treatment of Loyalists and was labeled the "bloody tyrant of Washington County." William Campbell died shortly after being promoted to brigadier general.

Archibald Cary (1721–1787) was a major landowner and politician. During the Revolutionary War, Cary was in charge of recruiting soldiers and procuring supplies in central Virginia. He built factories in Manchester and Richmond to produce gunpowder and rope. He lent money to Virginia to underwrite the cost of the Virginia militia (money that was never repaid). He was one of the commissioners who managed the move of the state government from Williamsburg to Richmond. An ardent supporter of the Anglican Church, Cary zealously pursued the arrest of Baptist preachers who preached without a license. Some of his contemporaries believed a story that after hearing talk that Patrick Henry might be appointed dictator of Virginia, Cary swore that if that happened he would then stab Patrick Henry to death.

Richard Dale (1756–1826) had a most unusual naval career. Born in Portsmouth, Virginia, Dale began his life at sea at the age of twelve aboard a merchant ship owned by his uncle. Over the course of the next several years, he crossed the Atlantic and made several trips to the West Indies. In 1776, he joined the Virginia Navy as a lieutenant but was soon captured by the tender ship of a British frigate. He knew many of the crew of this ship, and they persuaded him to join the British cause.

Sailing to the West Indies, the British ship on which Dale served was captured by the American ship USS *Lexington*. Dale enlisted as a midshipman aboard *Lexington*, which was, in turn, captured by HMS *Pearl* later in 1776. Dale was released as part of a prisoner exchange in January 1777 and returned to duty with an American squadron deployed off the coast of Ireland. Once again, Dale's ship was captured, and he and the rest of the crew were sent to Mill Prison in Plymouth, England.

The prisoners were treated harshly, so starved at one point that they were reduced to killing and eating a dog; they knew that they would probably die if they did not escape. The American sailors dug a tunnel under the wall of the prison. Dale was recaptured attempting to board a ship for France. He was returned to Mill Prison, where he remained until February 1779, when, having somehow procured the uniform of a British officer, he calmly walked out the gates of the prison. This time he reached France.

In France, Dale signed aboard the American privateer USS *Bonhomme Richard*, commanded by John Paul Jones. He was shortly promoted to first lieutenant. Dale remained Jones's first lieutenant for two years, bringing the war into British waters. Dale sailed into Philadelphia in 1781, the first time he had been on American soil in four years. Dale next sailed in the Continental navy ship USS *Trumbull*, which was captured almost as soon as it left Philadelphia.

Dale was a prisoner of war once again. Exchanged after two months, he next served on an American privateer before returning to Philadelphia in February 1783. The war officially ended in September 1783, the Continental navy was disbanded and Richard Dale became a civilian for the first time in eight years.

WILLIAM FLORA (1755–1818) was a free-born African American. As required by the Virginia Militia Law, shortly after his eighteenth birthday, Flora enrolled in the Princess Anne County Militia and met regularly for drill with his neighbors. Flora fought bravely in Colonel William Woodford's Second Virginia Regiment at the Battle of Great Bridge. He was one of several sentries stationed on the narrow bridge that divided the British and Patriot positions. The British attacked on the morning of December 8, 1775. Flora and the other sentries fired into the advancing redcoats, alerting Patriots manning the forward breastworks. After a few rounds were fired, the other sentries hastily retreated, but Flora stood and delivered eight more rounds, at one point engaging an entire British platoon singlehandedly, before retreating. Flora slowed the British advance, giving Patriot soldiers ample time to man their defenses. His valiant actions were praised by his comrades and even by a newspaper of the time. Later, Flora enlisted as a private in the Fifteenth Virginia Continental Regiment and served with this unit for three years until he was honorably discharged after the Battle of Yorktown. After the war, Flora became the owner of a livery stable in Portsmouth. He received a one-hundred-acre bounty land warrant for his service during the Revolutionary War.

PETER FRANCISCO (1760–1831) was six feet, eight inches tall and weighed some 260 pounds; he has come down through history with the title of the "Virginia Giant." His deeds during the Revolutionary War became the stuff of myth and legend. Some of the stories may actually contain an element of truth; others, if not true, "ought to be," in the words of the heroic storytellers of the Revolution. The stories of the Giant's deeds were so popular by the 1820s that the early Revolutionary War historian Alexander Garden wrote that he "scarcely ever met a man in Virginia who had not some miraculous tale to tell of Peter Francisco."

Pedro (later called Peter) Francisco arrived at the dock in City Point aged five, friendless and unable to speak English. It is believed that he had been kidnapped from his Portuguese parents in the Azores. He was taken in and raised by the family of Judge Anthony Winston.

In 1776, at the age of sixteen, Francisco enlisted in the Virginia Line. He fought in Pennsylvania at the Battle of Germantown and in New Jersey at the Battle of Monmouth. Francisco was part of an attack on the British fort of Stony Point in New York, where, supposedly, even after receiving a nine-inch wound to the stomach, he continued to fight, killing twelve British grenadiers and capturing the enemy's flag.

The story of "Francisco's Fight" relates how the legendary giant, although unarmed, overpowered nine of Banastre Tarleton's dragoons. *Courtesy of the Library of Congress.*

One of his most well-known feats occurred in South Carolina after the Battle of Camden. Seeing an American cannon mired in mud and about to be abandoned, he freed the 1,100-pound cannon and carried it on his shoulders to keep it from falling into the hands of the enemy.

He fought at Guilford Court House in North Carolina. A monument at Guilford Court House National Military Park commemorates Francisco's efforts: "To Peter Francisco a giant in stature, might, and courage who slew in this engagement eleven of the enemy with his own broad sword rendering himself thereby perhaps the most famous Private soldier of the Revolutionary War."

The story of "Francisco's Fight" relates how the legendary giant, although unarmed, overpowered nine of Banastre Tarleton's dragoons who were trying to rob him of the silver buckles on his shoes. He supposedly killed three dragoons and made off with eight horses.

PETER MUHLENBERG (1746–1807) was an ordained Lutheran pastor and an ordained Anglican minister serving a Lutheran community in Woodstock, Virginia. He was an ardent supporter of the Patriot cause. On January 21, 1776, in the Lutheran church in Woodstock, Reverend Muhlenberg read from the third chapter of Ecclesiastes, which starts with "To everything, there is a season…"; after reading the eighth verse, "a time of war, and a time of peace," he declared, "And this is the time of war." He then removed his black clerical robe to reveal his colonel's uniform. Within thirty minutes, 162 men enlisted. By the next day, Muhlenberg had recruited 300 men for the Eighth Virginia Regiment, which was made up primarily of German Americans.

In early 1777, the Eighth Virginia joined Washington's army in the north. Muhlenberg was promoted to brigadier general and given command of the entire Virginia Line. Muhlenberg fought at the Battles of Brandywine, Germantown and Monmouth. When the Virginia Line was sent to help defend Charlestown, South Carolina, Muhlenberg himself was ordered to Virginia to help repel the British invasion. During the Yorktown campaign, Muhlenberg served as a brigade commander in Lafayette's Division.

ROBERT CARTER III (1728–1804) was very active in colonial politics, sitting on the Governor's Council for some two decades. He effectively retired from public life in 1772 after the Governor's Council voted to allow slaveholders or local authorities to punish the enslaved without due process of law. In 1776, Carter took a loyalty oath but, despite the urgings of Patriot friends, declined official position. He began supplying provisions to Patriot forces.

During the war years, Carter underwent a spiritual awakening following a mystical experience. In 1778, Carter became a Baptist. He knew other men who had their lives threatened after conversion, and he had personally attended two different Baptist services before his conversion that were attacked by armed mobs. Carter further scandalized the neighborhood by joining a congregation that included free Blacks and the enslaved.

In the years after the Revolutionary War, some slaveholders in Virginia freed their slaves, often in their wills, and noted principles of equality and the ideals of the Revolution as the reason for their decisions. Carter hoped that Virginia would pass legislation enabling gradual emancipation, as was being done in New York and New Jersey, but began a personal program of gradual emancipation on his many plantations. His plan was resisted by family and neighbors, and he was shunned in the community. Nevertheless, he emancipated some five hundred people. This was the largest individual freeing of the enslaved before President Abraham Lincoln's Emancipation Proclamation.

STEPHEN TRIGG (1744–1782) was a member of the Fincastle County Committee of Safety, responding to the threat the Cherokees posed when they entered the war on the side of the British in 1776. The members of the Committee of Safety drafted a letter to the chiefs of the Cherokee Nation proposing a peace agreement. The letter stated, "It is true that an unhappy Difference hath subsisted between the people beyond the great water, and the Americans for some years, which was entirely Owing to some of the great Kings Servants who wanted to take Our money without Our Consent, and otherwise to treat us, not like Children, but Slaves, which the people of America will not submit to." The Cherokee did not respond to the peace overtures, and Trigg participated in a 1776–77 campaign to subdue the hostiles on Virginia's frontier.

In 1782, the British launched an invasion of Kentucky, which was then part of Virginia. The Battle of Blue Licks was fought on August 19, 1782, ten months after Lord Cornwallis surrendered at Yorktown. Fifty Loyalists and three hundred Native American warriors ambushed and routed the American militia. Trigg was killed, and his men fell back after only five minutes of battle.

DANIEL BOONE (1734–1820) served as a militia officer during the Revolutionary War, fighting in Kentucky, then the westernmost frontier of Virginia. Boone was elected to three terms in the Virginia General Assembly during the war.

He was captured in Charlottesville during Banastre Tarleton's 1781 raid on Charlottesville but was released as being a person of little importance. Boone fought in the Battle of Blue Licks in 1782, one of the last battles of the American Revolution.

In the Twilight of the Revolution

Perhaps the most venerated tomb in America is that of George Washington. Washington died on December 14, 1799. Congress resolved to build a marble monument in the new Capitol Building. Martha Washington granted her consent. A crypt was provided under the dome of the Capitol, but the project was never completed.

At ten o'clock at night on December 14, 1799, George Washington, fearing premature burial, requested of his doctors to be "decently buried" and to "not let my body be put into the Vault in less than three days after I am dead." In his last will, he expressed the desire to be buried at Mount Vernon.

George Washington was entombed in the existing family vault, now known as the Old Vault, on December 18, 1799. Visitors wrote that the tomb was "[a] low, obscure, ice house looking brick vault," which "testifies how well a Nation's gratitude repays the soldier's toils, the statesman's labors, the patriot's virtue, and the father's cares."

In his last will, George Washington directed the building of a new family burial vault in the following words: "The family Vault at Mount Vernon requiring repairs, and being improperly situated besides, I desire that a new one of Brick, and upon a larger Scale, may be built at the foot of what is commonly called the Vineyard Inclosure."

In 1831, Washington's body was transferred to the new tomb. A French visitor wrote that Mount Vernon had become "like Jerusalem and Mecca, the resort of the travelers of all nations who come within its vicinity." Visitors were filled with "veneration and respect," leading them "to make a pilgrimage to the shrine of patriotism and public worth." Pilgrims from across the country converged on Mount Vernon during the early nineteenth century. Veterans of the American Revolution connected deeply to Washington through the pilgrimage. Many pilgrims, overwhelmed with emotion, wept. An early diarist recounted the following: "One [man] placed himself on the green turf and mused, with his head resting on his arms.

People made pilgrimages to the tomb of George Washington, the great hero of the Revolution. *Courtesy of the Library of Congress.*

Another stood alone among the thicket with folded arms and downcast eyes. A third reclined against a tree and wept…there was nothing artificial in this, nothing premeditated."

The legend "Within this Enclosure Rest the remains of Genl. George Washington" is inscribed on a stone tablet over the entrance to the tomb. Behind an iron gate are two marble sarcophagi, one inscribed "Washington" and the other "Martha, Consort of Washington." The marble sarcophagus in which the body of General Washington now rests was erected in 1837. The remains of Martha Washington reside in a similar but plainer sarcophagus. After Washington's death, the sixty-eight-year-old Martha closed up the second-floor bedroom that she had shared with her husband and moved to a room on the third floor. She turned increasingly to religion, spending part of every day in religious study. One visitor remarked in 1801, "She speaks of death as a pleasant journey." Martha Washington died two and a half years after her husband on May 22, 1802.

Wreath-laying ceremonies have always been important and continue to be held daily by patriotic, civic and citizen's groups. Wreath-laying ceremonies consist of the Pledge of Allegiance, General Washington's prayer for his country and the placement of a wreath by no more than two participants within the locked tomb area. Some 1 million visitors view the tomb annually. George Washington's prayer for America reads as follows:

> *I now make it my earnest prayer, that God would have the United States in his holy protection, that he would incline the hearts of the Citizens to cultivate a spirit of subordination and obedience to Government, to entertain a brotherly affection and love for one another, for their fellow citizens of the United States at large, and particularly for their brethren who have served in the Field, and finally, that he would most graciously be pleased to dispose us all, to do Justice, to love mercy, and to demean ourselves with that Charity, humility and pacific temper of mind, which were the Characteristics of the Devine Author of our blessed Religion, and without an humble imitation of whose example in these things, we can never hope to be a happy Nation. Amen.*

SELECTED BIBLIOGRAPHY

Books

Brady, Patricia. *Martha Washington: An American Life*. New York: Penguin, 2006.

Bryan, Helen. *Martha Washington: First Lady of Liberty*. New York: John Wiley, 2002.

Cayton, M.K., E.J. Goran and P.W. Williams, eds. *Encyclopedia of American Social History*. Vol. 3. New York: Scribners, 1993.

Cecere, Michael. *A Universal Appearance of War: The Revolutionary War in Virginia, 1775–1781*. Berwyn Heights, MD: Heritage Books, 2014.

Cobbett, William, ed. *The Parliamentary History of England: From the Earliest Period to the Year 1803*. London, 1813.

Franklin, John H., and Loren Schweninger. *Runaway Slaves: Rebels on the Plantation*. New York: Oxford University Press, 1999.

Gaines, William H., ed. *A Hornbook of Virginia History*. Richmond: Virginia State Library, 1965.

Kennedy, John P., ed. *Journals of the House of Burgesses of Virginia, 1761–1765*. Richmond, VA, 1907.

Link, William A. *Roots of Secession: Slavery and Politics in Antebellum Virginia*. Chapel Hill: University of North Carolina Press, 2003.

Mitchell, Sarah E. *Men's Clothing, 1760–1785*. Chatham, VA: Mitchell Publications, 2012.

Munson, James D. *Col. John Carlyle, Gent*. Alexandria: Northern Virginia Park Authority, 1986.

Rutland, Robert, ed. *The Papers of George Mason, 1725–1792*. Vol. 1. Chapel Hill: University of North Carolina Press, 1970.

Schama, Simon. *Rough Crossing*. New York: HarperCollins, 2007.

Schwarz, Philip J. *Migrants Against Slavery: Virginians and the Nation*. Charlottesville: University Press of Virginia, 2001.

Selby, John E. *The Revolution in Virginia, 1775–1783*. Williamsburg, VA: Colonial Williamsburg Foundation, 1988.

Wiencek, Henry. *An Imperfect God: George Washington, His Slaves, and the Creation of America*. New York: Straus and Giroux, 2003.

Websites

Abraham Lincoln on Line. Letter to Henry L. Pierce and Others. www.abrahamlincolnonline.org/lincoln/speeches/pierce.htm.

American Battlefield Trust. https://www.battlefields.org.

Avoca Museum. "Colonel Charles Lynch." https://www.avocamuseum.org/col-charles-lynch.

Bilal, Kolby. "Black Pilots, Patriots, and Pirates: African-American Participation in the Virginia State and British Navies during the Revolutionary War in Virginia." College of William and Mary, 2000. Dissertations, Theses and Masters Projects. 1539626268. https://dx.doi.org/doi:10.21220/s2-4hv4-ds79.

Black Loyalist Heritage Society. www.blackloyalist.com.

Cecere, Michael. "The Rise of Virginia's Independent Militia." Journal of the American Revolution. allthingsliberty.com.

Colonial Williamsburg. "Give Me Liberty or Give Me Death!" colonialwilliamsburg.org.

Colvin, Alex. "Religious Liberty in Virginia: How 'Dissenters' Parlayed Oppression into Freedom." Journal of the American Revolution. allthingsliberty.com.

Daughters of the American Revolution. "Patriot Profiles—Honoring Our Patriots." dar.org.

Explore Southern History. "The Crossing of the Dan—Virginia & North Carolina." exploresouthernhistory.com.

Founders Online, National Archives. "The Diary of John Adams." December 17, 1773. archives.gov.

———. "Fairfax County Resolves, 18 July 1774." archives.gov.

———. "The Resolutions as Adopted by Congress, 31 July 1775." archives. gov.

Gallup, John. "The Equipment of the Virginia Soldier in the American Revolution." College of William and Mary, 1991. Dissertations, Theses and Masters Projects. 1539625655. https://dx.doi.org/doi:10.21220/s2-s7w6-xp43.

History of Loudon County, Virginia. "John Champe, a Revolutionary War Double Agent." loudounhistory.org.

Kerpelman, Larry C. "The Slave Who Spied: James Armistead's Role in Revolutionary War." historynet.com.

Lepore, Jill. "Goodbye, Columbus." *The New Yorker* (May 8, 2006). www. newyorker.com/magazine/2006/05/08/goodbye-columbus.

Monticello. www.monticello.org.

Mount Vernon. www.mountvernon.org.

National Archives. "The Virginia Declaration of Rights." https://www. archives.gov/founding-docs/virginia-declaration-of-rights.

Owen, Margaret Elizabeth. "Guarding the Other Frontier: The Virginia State Navy and Its Men, 1775–1783." College of William and Mary, 2009. Dissertations, Theses and Masters Projects. 1539626603. https:// dx.doi.org/doi:10.21220/s2-h8bw-vt40.

Virginia Museum of History and Culture. "American Revolution." virginiahistory.org.

Virginia Places. www.virginiaplaces.org.

INDEX

C

Camm, John 112
Campbell, Christiana 106
Campbell, William 123
Carlyle, John 11, 41, 76
Cary, Archibald 123
Catholics 68
Champe, Sergeant Major John 121, 122
Charles City County 41, 42, 105
Charlestown, South Carolina 35, 58, 90, 107, 108, 126
Charlotte County 42
Charlottesville 30, 39, 70, 99, 112, 117
Cherokee Nation 127
Chesapeake Bay 28, 32, 48, 96, 97
Chesterfield County 30
childbearing 76
Clark, George Rogers 28, 42
Coercive Acts 16
Cole, Thomas 92
Collier, Admiral Sir George 28, 116
Colonial Williamsburg 43, 44
Committee of Correspondence 14
Committee of Safety 20, 21, 88, 96
Conciliatory Resolution 18
Continental Congress 16, 18, 19, 21, 25, 27, 36, 83, 86, 88, 99, 100
Corbin, Hannah Lee 104
Cornwallis, Major General Charles Lord 30, 31, 32, 33, 34, 35, 36, 48, 58, 100, 101, 109, 116, 117, 127
cosmetics 72
courtship 73

Craik, Dr. James 39
Cresswell, Nicholas 41, 87
Culpeper County 99
Culpeper Minutemen 22, 23, 87
Custis, Daniel Parke 75, 118
Custis, Jacky 47, 112, 118, 119, 120, 121
Custis, Patsy 118, 119

D

Dale, Richard 123
dancing 72, 81
Declaration of Independence 28, 37, 42, 45, 59, 62, 98, 104
Dinwiddie County 93
divorce 77
Dragon 48, 95
dresses 66, 78
Dumfries 53, 99
Dunmore, John Murray, Earl of 15, 16, 17, 18, 20, 21, 22, 23, 24

E

Eastern State Hospital 50
education 41, 72, 75, 119
Elizabeth River 22
Ethiopian Regiment 21, 107

F

Fairfax, Bryan 115
Fairfax County 41, 43, 45, 46, 48, 86, 87

ABOUT THE AUTHOR

Chuck Mills has a passion for history. He has roamed the world researching historical topics and is delighted to have lived most of his life in Northern Virginia, one of the most historic regions in the country. He now lives on the banks of the Potomac River on land once owned by George Washington. Chuck is a graduate of Penn State University and has advanced degrees from Penn State and from George Washington University. He recently completed a master's degree in American history at George Mason University in Fairfax, Virginia. Chuck is a member of the Sons of the American Revolution, the Alexandria Historical Society and the Prince William Historic Preservation Society; a former member of the board of directors of the Manassas Museum; and has acted as a docent at the Carlyle House Historic Park in Alexandria. He is the author of *Hidden History of Northern Virginia*, *Echoes of Manassas*, *Historic Cemeteries of Northern Virginia* and *Virginia Legends and Lore* and has written numerous newspaper and magazine articles on historical subjects. Chuck is the producer and cohost of *Virginia Time Travel*, a history television show that airs to some 2 million viewers in Northern Virginia. When not doing genealogical or historical research, Chuck can be found kayaking on the Potomac River.

Visit us at
www.historypress.com